Palgrave Studies in International Relations

Series Editors
Mai'a K. Davis Cross
Northeastern University
Boston, MA, USA

Benjamin de Carvalho
Norwegian Institute of International Affairs
Oslo, Norway

Shahar Hameiri
University of Queensland
St. Lucia, QLD, Australia

Knud Erik Jørgensen
University of Aarhus
Aarhus, Denmark

Ole Jacob Sending
Norwegian Institute of International Affairs
Oslo, Norway

Ayşe Zarakol
University of Cambridge
Cambridge, UK

Palgrave Studies in International Relations (the EISA book series), published in association with European International Studies Association, provides scholars with the best theoretically-informed scholarship on the global issues of our time. The series includes cutting-edge monographs and edited collections which bridge schools of thought and cross the boundaries of conventional fields of study. EISA members can access a 50% discount to PSIR, the EISA book series, here http://www.eisa-net. org/sitecore/content/be-bruga/mci-registrations/eisa/login/land-ing.aspx.

Mai'a K. Davis Cross is the Edward W. Brooke Professor of Political Science at Northeastern University, USA, and Senior Researcher at the ARENA Centre for European Studies, University of Oslo, Norway.

Benjamin de Carvalho is a Senior Research Fellow at the Norwegian Institute of International Affairs (NUPI), Norway.

Shahar Hameiri is Associate Professor of International Politics and Associate Director of the Graduate Centre in Governance and International Affairs, School of Political Science and International Studies, University of Queensland, Australia.

Knud Erik Jørgensen is Professor of International Relations at Aarhus University, Denmark, and at Yaşar University, Izmir, Turkey.

Ole Jacob Sending is the Research Director at the Norwegian Institute of International Affairs (NUPI), Norway.

Ayşe Zarakol is Reader in International Relations at the University of Cambridge and a fellow at Emmanuel College, UK.

More information about this series at
http://www.palgrave.com/gp/series/14619

Sofia Stolk • Renske Vos
Editors

International Law's Collected Stories

Editors
Sofia Stolk
T.M.C. Asser Instituut /
University of Amsterdam
The Hague, The Netherlands

Renske Vos
VU Amsterdam
Amsterdam, The Netherlands

Palgrave Studies in International Relations
ISBN 978-3-030-58834-2   ISBN 978-3-030-58835-9   (eBook)
https://doi.org/10.1007/978-3-030-58835-9

This Palgrave Macmillan imprint is published by the registered company Springer Nature Switzerland AG.
The registered company address is: Gewerbestrasse 11, 6330 Cham, Switzerland

About the Book

This edited volume presents a collection of stories that experiment with different ways of looking at international law. By using different literary lenses–namely, storytelling, the novel, the drama, the collage, the self-portrait, and the museum–the authors shed light on elements of international law that usually remain unseen or unheard and expose the limits of what international law can do. We inquire into who the storytellers of international law are, the stages on which they tell their stories, and who are absent in these tales. We present it as a collection: a set of chapters that more or less deal with the same subject matter. Alternatively, we would like to call it a potpourri of stories, since the diversity of topics and approaches is eclectic and unconventional. By placing multiple perspectives alongside each other we aim to compare and contrast, to allow for second thoughts, and to rediscover. In doing so, we engage with the ambiguities of international law's characters and spaces, and with the worldviews they reflect and worlds they create.

CONTENTS

Notes on Contributors

Thomas Charman is a postdoctoral fellow at the Institute for Advanced Studies in the Humanities, University of Edinburgh.

Mark Drumbl is the Class of 1975 Alumni Professor at Washington and Lee University, School of Law.

Owen Zong-Syuan Han is an LLM student at the National Taiwan University.

Miha Marčenko is a PhD candidate at the T.M.C. Asser Instituut / University of Amsterdam.

Aoife O'Leary McNeice is a PhD candidate in the Faculty of History, University of Cambridge.

Lisa Roodenburg is a PhD candidate at the T.M.C. Asser Instituut / University of Amsterdam.

Elisabeth Schweiger is an associate lecturer in the Department of Politics, York University.

Gerry Simpson is Professor of Public International Law at the London School of Economics and Political Science.

Sofia Stolk is a researcher in International Law at the T.M.C. Asser Instituut / University of Amsterdam.

Renske Vos is a lecturer and researcher in the Department of Transnational Legal Studies at VU Amsterdam.

LIST OF FIGURES

CHAPTER 1

Once Upon a Time in International Law…

Sofia Stolk and Renske Vos

In international law, we tell stories all the time, both within law and without.[1] Like all people, lawyers and legal scholars are storytellers. As human beings, telling stories is how we seek meaning.[2] This volume presents a collection of stories, as an effort to make sense of international law, to critique its dominant form and to recognize and explore its fundamentally literary character. It inquires into who the storytellers of international law are, where the stages on which they tell their stories are found, and who are absent from these tales. We present it as a collection: a set of different chapters that more or less deal with the same subject matter. Alternatively,

---

[1] James Boyd White, *Heracles' Bow: Essays on the Rhetoric and Poetics of the Law* (Wisconsin: The University of Wisconsin Press, 1985), 169; Gerry Simpson, 'The Sentimental Life of International Law,' *London Review of International Law*, 3, no. 1 (2015): 3–29.

[2] Ibid. White. On the relation between stories and identity in general see Clifford Geertz, *The Interpretation of Cultures: Selected Essays,* vol. 5019 (NY: Basic books, 1973).

S. Stolk
T.M.C. Asser Instituut / University of Amsterdam, The Hague, The Netherlands
e-mail: s.stolk@asser.nl

R. Vos (✉)
VU Amsterdam, Amsterdam, The Netherlands
e-mail: r.n.vos@vu.nl

© The Author(s), under exclusive license to Springer Nature Switzerland AG 2020
S. Stolk, R. Vos (eds.), *International Law's Collected Stories*, Palgrave Studies in International Relations, https://doi.org/10.1007/978-3-030-58835-9_1

we would like to call it a *potpourri of stories*, since the diversity of topics and approaches is an eclectic and unconventional mix. By placing multiple perspectives alongside each other we aim to compare and contrast, to allow for second thoughts, and to rediscover. In doing so, we engage with the ambiguities of international law's characters and spaces, and with the worldviews they reflect and worlds they create.[3]

The idea of this volume is to experiment with alternative literary forms as lenses through which to look anew at international law and to find what doors this may open. In this way, we aim to expose the limits as well as the possibilities or 'surplus' of international law in a playful yet reflexive way. In so doing, we take Gerry Simpson's plea for a sentimental international law to heart, and carry:

> an attentiveness to the unseen and unheard or, seemingly, insubstantial or a commitment to an international law of style and love and smallness, and an attentiveness to the everyday and to the informalities of power.[4]

There is not just one way in which the story of international law can be told. To cite White: 'to tell a story is to choose a language in which it is to be told, and to choose a language is, at some level, to recognize that there are other possible languages, other possible meanings.'[5] This is the main driver behind this book: a curiosity about these other possibilities and a strong belief in the need for experimentation and creativity to push our boundaries of imagining and enacting international law.

Law bears an undeniable yet uncomfortable relation to stories. Lawyers are, perhaps more than anyone, aware that storytelling is part and parcel

---

[3] For an interesting analysis of the stories that international (legal) institutions tell about themselves, see Martti Koskenniemi, 'The Preamble of the Universal Declaration of Human Rights,' in *The Universal Declaration of Human Rights: A Common Standard of Achievement*, eds. G. Alfredsson & A. Eide (Leiden: Martinus Nijhoff Publishers, 1999). On the construction of a narrative of international criminal courts specifically, see Sara Kendall and Sarah Nouwen, 'Representational Practices at the International Criminal Court: The Gap between Juridified and Abstract Victimhood,' *Law and Contemporary Problems* 76 (2013): 235; Christine Schwobel-Patel, 'The Comfort of International Criminal Law,' *Law and Critique* 24 (2013): 169; Sofia Stolk, '"The Records on Which History Will Judge Us Tomorrow": Auto-History in the Opening Statements of International Criminal Trials,' *Leiden Journal of International Law*, 28, no. 4 (2015): 993–1012. For a similar account in the EU context, see Renske Vos, *Europe and the Sea of Stories* (PhD thesis, VU Amsterdam, 2020).

[4] Simpson (n 1): 28.

[5] White (n 1): 174.

of the profession. At the same time, the term 'story' seems at odds with law's presumed solemnity and objectivity. Storytelling connotes a degree of freedom and imagination, while legal language is typified as strict and as a 'boring' genre, marked by dry technocratic terms. For the larger part, any field of law is rather static and predictable in its use of language, limited by a narrow understanding of what is recognized as acceptable within the discourse of the discipline. In the words of Yahyaoui Krivenko: 'By limiting the acceptable styles and usages of language, international law limits the number and nature of acceptable arguments. Therefore, despite a relatively broad range of possible outcomes available and the potential open-endedness of international law, the stylistic conventions of international law as a discipline exclude and thus significantly limit the number of acceptable avenues and outcomes.'[6] For international law, the stylistic conservatism of its legal language clashes with another discourse that is foundational to its existence: the discourse of justice. International law seems to encounter problems with properly capturing the sensitivity of the dramatic subject matter it deals with in its limited vocabulary, and risks becoming simplistic, stereotypical, or overly technical.[7]

Still, the literary character of law has long been recognized. International law has been understood as a kind of language, as an argumentative practice, or, although rarely, as literary activity.[8] More broadly speaking, the question of the relation between law and arts dates back comfortably to

---

[6] Ekatarina Yahyaoui Krivenko, 'International law, literature and interdisciplinarity,' *Law and Humanities*, 9, no. 1 (2015): 120.

[7] See, for example, Simpson (n 1); Christine Schwöbel, 'The 'Ideal' Victim of International Criminal Law,' *European Journal of International Law*, 29, no. 3 (2018); Yahyaoui Krivenko (n 6): 122; Martha Nussbaum, *Political Emotions: Why Love Matters for Justice* (Cambridge, MA: Belknap, 2013).

[8] Some examples include David Kennedy, *A World of Struggle: How Power, Law, and Expertise Shape Global Political Economy* (Princeton: Princeton University Press, 2018); Ingo Venzke, *How interpretation makes international law: on semantic change and normative twists* (Oxford: OUP, 2012); Wouter Werner, 'Recall it again, Sam. Practices of Repetition in the Security Council,' *Nordic Journal of International Law* 86, no. 2 (2017): 151–169; Christopher Warren, *Literature and the Law of Nations, 1580–1680* (Oxford: OUP, 2015); Lianne Boer, 'Narratives of Force: The Presence of the Writer in International Legal Scholarship,' *Netherlands International Law Review* 66, no. 1 (2019): 1–20; Edward Morgan, *Aesthetics of International Law* (Toronto: University of Toronto Press, 2007); Raimond Gaita, 'Literature, Genocide, and the Philosophy of International Law,' in *Crime, Punishment and Responsibility* eds. Rowan Cruft, Matthew Kramer & Mark Reiff (Oxford: OUP, 2011).

antiquity.[9] Though it has been held that 'we live in a period in which it is harder to unite literature, myth, theatre, law and political life than it was,' it is equally alleged that there might also be an emerging tendency to (re) unite them.[10] Efforts in the field of International Relations to involve aesthetics in a 'search for thinking space: to explore ever new ways of writing, seeing, hearing and sensing the political'[11] have sparked engagement with cultural forms as varying as novels,[12] poetry,[13] colour,[14] and cartoons.[15] Such explorations have also carried over to international law, as attested for by the latter discipline's extending inquiry into, for example,

[9] Emiliano Buis, 'How to Play Justice and Drama in Antiquity: Law and Theatre in Athens as Performative Rituals,' *Florida Journal of International Law* (2004); Jaqueline Mowbray, *Linguistic Justice: International Law and Language Policy* (Oxford: OUP, 2012).

[10] Simpson (n 1).

[11] Roland Bleiker, 'In Search of Thinking Space: Reflections on the Aesthetic Turn in International Political Theory,' *Millennium* 45, no. 2 (2017): 258–264.

[12] Elizabeth Dauphinee, *The Politics of Exile* (London: Routledge, 2013); Jenny Edkins, 'Novel Writing in International Relations: Openings for a Creative Practice,' *Security Dialogue* 44, no. 4 (2013): 281–297.

[13] Louiza Odysseos, 'Prolegomena to Any Future Decolonial Ethics: Coloniality, Poetics and "Being Human as Praxis,"' *Millennium* 45, no. 3 (2017): 447–72.

[14] Xavier Guillaume, Rune Andersen, Juha Vuori, 'Paint it black: Colours and the social meaning of the battlefield,' *European Journal of International Relations* 22, no. 1 (2015): 49–71.

[15] Kyle Grayson, 'How to Read Paddington Bear: Liberalism and the Foreign Subject in *A Bear Called Paddington*,' *British Journal of Politics and International Relations* 15, no. 3 (2013): 378–393.

narratives,[16] painting,[17] fashion,[18] photography,[19] architecture,[20] film,[21] theatre,[22] sound,[23] objects,[24] and comic books.[25]

It is within the burgeoning yet sometimes inherently paradoxical fields of international law and literature or aesthetics that we loosely situate the collected stories presented in this book, without taking up a fixed position in the law and/as/in literature debate.[26] Rather, we aim to contribute to a type of international legal scholarship that, in the words of Hohmann and Joyce, aims to 'disrupt established disciplinary techniques, boundaries, and hierarchies.'[27] We pivot this on an approach that is not only critiquing but also alluring, by (re)discovering new styles of reading and writing international law that are disruptive yet that sparkle. This is in order to contest and resist thinking in and about international law in a dogmatic language, but also to emphasize that it is within international law itself that we may find alternative ways of telling stories about it. To

---

[16] Surabhi Ranganathan, 'The Value of Narratives: The India-USA Nuclear Deal in Terms of Fragmentation, Pluralism, Constitutionalisation and Global Administrative Law,' *Erasmus Law Review* 6, no.17 (2013).

[17] Sarah-Jane Koulen 'Blind Justice and the Portraits on the Wall' in *Illuminating the Backstage of Transnational Legal Practice* eds. Lianne Boer and Sofia Stolk (London: Routledge, 2019).

[18] Rose Parfitt, 'The Anti-Neutral Suit: International Legal Futurists, 1914–2017,' *London Review of International Law* 5, no. 1 (2017): 87–123.

[19] Luis Eslava, 'Istanbul Vignettes: Observing the Everyday Operation of International Law,' *London Review of International Law* 2, no. 1 (2014): 3–47.

[20] Sofia Stolk and Renske Vos (eds.) 'Special section: Brutal International Law: A Walk through Marcel Breuer's former American Embassy in The Hague,' *New Perspectives* 28, no. 1 (2020).

[21] Immi Tallgren, 'Watching Tokyo Trial,' *London Review of International Law* 5, no. 2 (2017): 291–316; Wouter Werner, '"We Cannot Allow Ourselves to Imagine What It All Means": Documentary Practices and the International Criminal Court,' *Law and Contemporary Problems* (2014): 76, 319.

[22] Julie Stone Peters, 'Legal Performance Good and Bad,' *Law, Culture and the Humanities* 4 (2008): 179–200; Mark Drumbl in this volume.

[23] James Parker, *Acoustic Jurisprudence: Listening to the Trial of Simon Bikindi* (Oxford: OUP, 2015).

[24] Hohmann and Joyce (n 27).

[25] Special Issue 'Seeing Law: The Comic and Icon as Law,' *International Journal for the Semiotics of Law/Revue Internationale de Sémiotique Juridique* 30, no. 3 (2017).

[26] If anything, we would like to pick up on the challenge of Megan Daigle 'to engage in that what we study: literary, novelistic forms of writing' in Megan Daigle 'Writing the Lives of Others: Storytelling and International Politics,' *Millennium* 45, no. 1 (2016): 25–42.

[27] Hohmann and Joyce (n 27): 6.

use the term 'story' does not aim to label the material in this volume 'unreal,' or to emphasize its non-legal character or to position it outside of the legal discourse. To the contrary, the analyses in this volume affirm that these stories are 'not an uncharacteristic, but a quintessential part' of what we call international law.[28]

Even so, in international law not all stories can be told. Law demands a certain form, and demands stories to fit within that form. As a consequence, not everything is told in law; not everyone's voice is heard. Because of law's considerations of what counts as relevant and its allocation of space to speak, law can erase, morph, silence, and 'un'-tell stories as much as it creates them.[29] Exposing international law's political agenda and its potential—or even design—as a tool of oppression is extensively discussed and criticized, particularly in the Third World Approaches to International Law (TWAIL) literature.[30] In this contribution, we ask what happens to the story of international law and who tells it when we change the form. We ask this partly in order to expose and challenge international law's underlying tensions and assumptions, and partly to play with and to contemplate alternatives by changing its literary register.

Using different lenses enables the authors in this volume to direct our attention in different ways. Contributors experiment with stories viewed

---

[28] Sofia Stolk, *The Opening Statement of the Prosecution in International Criminal Trials: A Solemn Tale of Horror* (London: Routledge, forthcoming 2021).

[29] Yahyaoui Krivenko (n 6): 113. On silence and silencing in international law, see Elisabeth Schweiger, 'Listen Closely: What Silence Can Tell Us About Legal Knowledge Production,' *London Review of International Law* 6, no. 3 (2018); Dianne Otto, 'Beyond legal justice: some personal reflections on people's tribunals, listening and responsibility,' *London Review of International Law* 5, no. 2 (2017): 225–249. More broadly, see: Gayatri Spivak, *Can the subaltern speak?* (London: Palgrave Macmillan, 1988); Lene Hansen, 'The Little Mermaid's Silent Security Dilemma and the Absence of Gender in the Copenhagen School,' *Millennium* 29, no. 2 (2000): 285–306; Xavier Guillaume, 'How to do things with silence: Rethinking the centrality of speech to the securitization framework,' *Security Dialogue* 49, no. 6 (2018): 476–492.

[30] See, for example, Anne Orford (ed.) *International Law and its Others* (Cambridge: CUP 2009); Rose Parfitt, *The Process of International Legal Reproduction: Inequality, Historiography, Resistance* (Cambridge: CUP, 2019); Luis Eslava, Michael Fakhri, and Vasuki Nesiah (eds.) *Bandung, global history, and international law: Critical pasts and pending futures* (Cambridge: CUP, 2017); Antony Anghie, 'The Evolution of International Law: colonial and postcolonial realities,' *Third World Quarterly* 27, no. 5 (2006): 740; Luis Eslava and Sundhya Pahuja, 'Beyond the (Post)Colonial: TWAIL and the Everyday Life of International Law,' *Journal of Law and Politics in Africa, Asia and Latin America* 45, no. 2 (2012): 206.

through literary lenses: novel, play, storytelling, portrait, collage, and museum. The book presents a collection of chapters, which in combined form reflect a kaleidoscope of stories told in international law, a picture book of international legal stages, and an assemblage of storytellers. From the outset, however, we want to make clear that this is indeed only a *collection* of possible stories, inherently limited and incomplete. This book too suffers from selectivity, displayed, for example, by its narrow geographical scope and the particular set of lenses chosen from an infinite pool of possibilities. That said, we propose that this book is an invitation rather than an end product. An invitation that has been taken up in an exciting variety of ways by the contributing authors.

THE COLLECTION

Elisabeth Schweiger and Aoife O'Leary McNeice take up the novel as a lens through which to look at international law. Specifically, their chapter illustrates different dynamics of silencing and exclusion in international law, by drawing on Jane Austen's infamous novel *Pride and Prejudice*. They open the door to see beyond a romanticized ideal of international law. Similar to international law, they contend, 'Jane Austen novels have been critiqued for representing an orientalist class society, in which the main characters tend to be white and upper-class, moving within a bubble of power and privilege.'[31] Through an engagement with Austen's intricate play of ambiguity and silence, the chapter seeks to redress interpretations of who is allowed to speak, be listened to, and be silent, in international law. In this way the subtleties of the novel serve to bring out the crudities in international law. The chapter moreover prepares the ground for an inquiry into international law's silences, by asking what stories cannot be told by or in international law.

Mark Drumbl takes the theatre play 'Kapo in Jerusalem' as his point of departure, engaging with the figure of the Kapo straddling the binary divide between victim and perpetrator. Through 75 monologues the play offers intimate and contrasting accounts of Bruno, a former Kapo in Auschwitz, who seeks to have his actions, himself, be understood, presenting his choices as rational, lesser evils. Yet as Drumbl reflects, '[w]hat 'understanding' actually would entail remains very unclear,'[32] and the

---

[31] Schweiger and O'Leary McNeice, Chap. 2 in this volume: 17.
[32] Drumbl, Chap. 3 in this volume: 46.

viewer is left not quite knowing what to make of the character.[33] This ambiguity is reflected on by characters in the play. One character is placed in the position of having to 'judge' Bruno in an administrative proceeding, yet he finds himself unable to do so. Drumbl notes how this inability to decide 'reflects law's struggles to come to terms with the Kapo.'[34] Still the character recommends law to go forward, when he personally found law unhelpful. To acquit Bruno is as reductive as to convict him. The play demonstrates the enduring pull of the law, beyond where the ability of the law to settle disputes reaches its limits. 'The hunger for law fails to satiate. "We" crave law, yet law leaves "us" unfilled and unfulfilled.'[35] As the staged play offers a space for the ambiguity of the figure of the Kapo to crystallize, it becomes evident why this figure cannot be captured within the space of the trial, where a suspect has to be placed on either side of the victim/perpetrator binary and cannot transcend it.

Thomas Charman picks up on another character that is difficult to place within the binaries of international (criminal) law: he tells the story of the male victim of sexual violence in armed conflict. This character falls victim to a double bind. First there is an undertold story of men as victim rather than perpetrator of sexual violence. This then feeds into a second under-told story in which this violence when it occurs is rather told as torture than rape. The chapter shows that the stories that *are* told make it increasingly difficult for other stories to also be told. Moreover, the space of the trial conceives of actions as either torture or rape. Charman explains how 'the telling of these stories as torture, or as instances of cruel and inhuman treatment, may represent a more reliable route to a conviction.'[36] On the one hand, it is commendable that perpetrators are convicted at all; on the other hand, what is being erased is the possibility to tell the story of these crimes as rape in court. So besides recognizing the nature of the violence or creating a space for the experiences of victims, there is also a legal reason for and consequence of telling a story in a particular way. This legal rationale might be in tension with these other objectives, but these alternative stories cannot (can no longer) be told in the space of the trial. It is then not just that legal language can suppress alternative meanings and narratives of what occurred, but that pushing for a conviction requires it.

---

[33] Ibid.
[34] Ibid: 47.
[35] Ibid: 49.
[36] Charman, Chap. 4 in this volume: 72.

This opens up many routes of further enquiry about the stories that are told and cannot be told and the ones that are silenced.

Moving from individual stories to the (un)told stories about larger entities, Lisa Roodenburg and Sofia Stolk engage with the presentation of The Hague and Amsterdam as international law cities through the lens of the self-portrait. Through this lens they seek to explore the association with international law as 'a matter of image building' beyond its function as 'cold' branding strategy, in order to shed light on 'the variety of motives and desires that are involved in a city's image building practices.'[37] Through interviews with the actors 'behind the scenes' working at the municipalities of Amsterdam and The Hague, they expose how the self-image is 'made, used and reinterpreted continuously.'[38] Their analysis reveals the challenge of building a city image that desires to target both an internal and external audience. In analogy with the self-portrait, these image building practices are both an exercise in self-reflection and a tool of outward communication. Their data shows the struggle of municipality staff to remedy the tension between different motives, desires, purposes, and intended audiences of the international law image, and reveals the complex and messy background to the cities' ostensibly straightforward attempts to enforce their affiliations with international law.

Miha Marčenko takes a further look at the city, and observes a similar multiplicity of actors behind what is presented as a uniform idea of a city's role and responsibilities. He zooms in on the 'ideal city,' a UN-based effort to construct a shared global vision of the city governed by international legal norms and principles.[39] By studying this effort through the lens of the collage, he destabilizes the idea of a harmonious trajectory and sheds light on the complexity of the processes, actors, and discourses involved. The collage lens enables us to see beyond the picture as a whole and shifts our gaze to its individual parts. In a collage, we can still distinguish traces of the origins of its building blocks and the transformations they underwent in the artist's act of reassembling. Looking at the ideal city as a collage illuminates the unresolved tensions and plurality of views and their constitutive role in the construction of the 'shared' view. Moreover, it emphasizes that the end product is made through selection: not all pieces get to be included in the collage. By drawing our attention

---

[37] Roodenburg and Stolk, Chap. 5 in this volume: 81.
[38] Ibid: 93.
[39] Marčenko, Chap. 6 in this volume: 97.

to the messiness and multiplicity of voices behind the ideal city, Marčenko also signals the ongoing process of amplification on the one hand and suppression of certain voices on the other. The collage thus shows the heterogeneous origins of the ideal city, disrupts a linear interpretation of its conception, but also stresses consideration of what is left out of the picture.

Renske Vos and Owen Zong-syuan Han explore the interaction between the maker and the recipients of a story in their empirical account of a study trip to the Jing-Mei White Terror Memorial Park and its accompanying National Human Rights Museum in Taipei, the site of a former prison and military court for political dissidents. They ask what the museum, and particularly the guided tour, can show or tell that international law cannot. The chapter describes an encounter between a 'carefully designed story' and a group of students with mixed national backgrounds and knowledge of human rights and Taiwanese history. Photos and student accounts give a unique insight into the process of making sense of law and history and show how the visitors' interpretations are shaped by the interaction between the museum's narrative and their own backgrounds and beliefs. The lens sheds a new light on the 'competing views of Taiwan's history and future' in the context of international law and human rights. It illuminates how the museum tour might be seen as a 'form of alternative diplomacy' seeking to confirm and communicate Taiwan's international sovereign status via cultural and educational channels.[40] Simultaneously, the empirical material reveals how such encounters open up additional space for reflection on and contestation of national histories and international law alike.

Finally, Gerry Simpson, takes up the epilogue to the volume as lens to review his own epilogual practices. He offers these ultimate reflections amidst the disruptive context of the cross-border incursions between law and literature from where international lawyers tell their tales.

A Mélange of Unconventional Approaches

These collected stories turn out to be surprisingly dark fairy tales. In some ways, they read like a Brothers Grimm tale, where the promise of beauty and wonder always comes with the infliction of violence.[41] What these

---

[40] Vos and Han, Chap. 7 in this volume: 117, 121.

[41] Maria Tatar, *The Hard Facts of the Grimms' Fairy Tales* (Princeton: Princeton University Press, 2nd edition 2003).

chapters are doing resembles, in the words of Simpson, the work of poets: 'to notice the micro-political humiliations that might entirely undercut the grand humanitarian scheme.'[42] In these elegies the dirt of the everyday adds depth to the complexity of law. In juxtaposition with an international law of ideals, glamour, and glorification,[43] these chapters in different forms expose difficulty, struggle, and vulnerability.[44]

The collected stories in this volume display a certain degree of intimacy and a sensitivity to human compassion. They invite the reader not only to be a spectator but to participate in the exercise of (ex)changing perspectives. Drumbl speaks of how stories can 'ferment in the minds of readers.' Using different literary lenses allows for the truth to be approached from multiple angles and for engagement with experiences that do not fit in more traditional types of scholarly writing. What is the legal validity of a city's branding strategy, or of a visit to a museum? Yet these cultivate crucial encounters for fostering international law's imaginary.[45] As such, this collection is a plea to listen to the undertold stories and usually unheard storytellers, to listen in on unlikely places.[46]

Paradoxically, changing the form in which a story of law is told draws awareness to the parameters of the form of law more commonly used. What is lost if international law translates highly personal experiences into its standard categories, and what is gained? Thomas Charman shows how certain stories are lost in court as a result of the path law stipulates in pursuing a conviction. Miha Marčenko questions the linearity that processes

---

[42] Simpson (n 1): 28.

[43] Immi Tallgren, 'Stardust of Justice? Celebrity in and by International Law,' research paper prepared for the Law and Society Association Annual Meeting 2018, on file with authors; Payam Akhavan, 'Making Human Rights Sexy: Authenticity in Glamorous Times' (*Harvard Human Rights Journal Blog*, 9 November 2012) <http://harvardhrj.com/2012/11/making-human-rights-sexy-authenticity-in-glamorous-times/> accessed on 25 June 2018.

[44] Luis Eslava, *Local Space, Global Life: The Everyday Operation of International Law and Development* (Cambridge: CUP, 2015); Fleur Johns, *Non-Legality in International Law: Unruly Law* (Cambridge: CUP 2013); Mikael Madsen, 'Sociological Approaches to International Courts,' *The Oxford Handbook of International Adjudication* eds. Romano et al (Oxford: OUP, 2015); Sarah Nouwen, 'As You Set out for Ithaka: Practical, Epistemological, Ethical, and Existential Questions about Socio-Legal Empirical Research in Conflict,' *Leiden Journal of International Law* 27 (2017): 227.

[45] Sofia Stolk and Renske Vos, 'International Legal Sightseeing,' *Leiden Journal of International Law* 33, no.1 (2020): 1.

[46] Schweiger and O'Leary McNeice (n 31): 18.

of law-making presume. He shows how the global governance ambitions for an 'ideal city' are marked by bringing and taking and rearranging. The chapters in this volume show what the legal—illegal binary of law cannot do justice to. They show that there is a limit to what can be said or staged within the space of international law. Yet equally they show that these limitations nonetheless do not quench the thirst for law. The pull of law remains, perhaps exactly because of its binary simplicity.

Whereas the collection shows how we can successfully draw parallels between law and art, they are ultimately not the same. This is not to say that law is real and theatre or paintings are not. Rather, it is to reiterate that there are things that one can stage in a play or transfer through a painting that one cannot achieve in court or at international conventions. There are things we cannot expect law to do. A trial is geared towards a verdict, which is by definition binary; a play can allow for multiple interpretations, offer nuance and accept inconclusiveness and confusion. To take the route of international law is to cut off alternative conceptions and consequences. This is what international law *must* do. But to do justice to international law in all its complexities and ambiguities, we need other lenses. To reconsider what international law is and does, the stories in this volume begin with what law leaves out.

After compiling this mélange of unconventional approaches to international law one thing stands out: sometimes law is better told outside of law. Therefore, this volume can be seen as an attempt to open up a space for a dialogue that is polyphonic, interdisciplinary, and multimodal.[47] Because changing lenses can make us see anew. This also means that this collection is by definition unfinished, and that it actually will never be complete. Since 'stories are always incomplete, always unfolding' they are in a process of 'constant adjustment and revision.'[48] In that sense, the

---

[47] M. Arvidsson and M. Bak McKenna, 'The Turn to History in International Law and the Sources Doctrine: Critical Approaches and Methodological Imaginaries' 33(1) *Leiden Journal of International Law* (2020) 37–56; N. Rajkovic, 'Interdisciplinarity' in J. d'Aspremont and S. Singh (eds.) *Concepts for International Law* (Elgar 2019); L. Boer and S. Stolk (eds.) *Illuminating the Backstage of Transnational Legal Practice* (Routledge, 2019); D. Lisle and H. Johnson, 'Lost in the Aftermath' 50(1) *Security Dialogue* (2018) 20–39; R. Saugmann, 'Military techno-vision: Technologies between visual ambiguity and the desire for security facts' 4 *European Journal of International Security* (2019) 300–321; B. Tallis' 'Multiplicity: Taking Responsibility for The International' 27(3) *New Perspectives* (2019) 166.

[48] White, p. 170.

book is an invitation to keep telling stories about international law and to keep disrupting them, both within law and without.

BIBLIOGRAPHY

Anghie, Antony. 2006. The Evolution of International Law: Colonial and Postcolonial Realities. *Third World Quarterly* 27 (5): 740–753.

Arvidsson, Matilda, and Miriam Bak McKenna. 2020. The Turn to History in International Law and the Sources Doctrine: Critical Approaches and Methodological Imaginaries. *Leiden Journal of International Law* 33 (1): 37–56.

Bleiker, Roland. 2017. In Search of Thinking Space: Reflections on the Aesthetic Turn in International Political Theory. *Millennium: Journal of International Studies* 45 (2): 258–264.

Boer, Lianne J.M. 2019. Narratives of Force: The Presence of the Writer in International Legal Scholarship. *Netherlands International Law Review* 66 (1): 1–20.

Boer, Lianne J.M., and Sofia Stolk, eds. 2019. *Illuminating the Backstage of Transnational Legal Practice*. London: Routledge.

Buis, Emiliano. 2004. How to Play Justice and Drama in Antiquity: Law and Theatre in Athens as Performative Rituals. *Florida Journal of International Law* 16: 697.

Daigle, Megan. 2016. Writing the Lives of Others: Storytelling and International Politics. *Millennium* 45 (1): 25–42.

Dauphinee, Elizabeth. 2013. *The Politics of Exile*. London: Routledge.

Edkins, Jenny. 2013. Novel Writing in International Relations: Openings for a Creative Practice. *Security Dialogue* 44 (4): 281–297.

Eslava, Luis. 2014. Istanbul Vignettes: Observing the Everyday Operation of International Law. *London Review of International Law* 2 (1): 3–47.

———. 2015. *Local Space, Global Life: The Everyday Operation of International Law and Development*. Cambridge: Cambridge University Press.

———. 2017. In *Bandung, Global History, and International Law: Critical Pasts and Pending Futures*, ed. Michael Fakhri and Vasuki Nesiah. Cambridge: Cambridge University Press.

Eslava, Luis, and Sundhya Pahuja. 2012. Beyond the (Post)Colonial: TWAIL and the Everyday Life of International Law. *Journal of Law and Politics in Africa, Asia and Latin America* 45 (2): 206.

Gaita, Raimmond. 2011. Literature, Genocide, and the Philosophy of International Law. In *Crime, Punishment and Responsibility*, ed. Rowan Cruft, Matthew Kramer, and Mark Reiff. Oxford: Oxford University Press.

Geertz, Clifford. 1973. *The Interpretation of Cultures: Selected Essays*. New York: Basic Books.

Grayson, Kyle. 2013. How to Read Paddington Bear: Liberalism and the Foreign Subject in *A Bear Called Paddington.* ' *British Journal of Politics and International Relations* 15 (3): 378–393.

Guillaume, Xavier. 2018. How to Do Things with Silence: Rethinking the Centrality of Speech to the Securitization Framework. *Security Dialogue* 49 (6): 476–492.

Guillaume, Xavier, Rune Andersen, and Juha Vuori. 2015. Paint It Black: Colours and the Social Meaning of the Battlefield. *European Journal of International Relations* 22 (1): 49–71.

Hansen, Lene. 2000. The Little Mermaid's Silent Security Dilemma and the Absence of Gender in the Copenhagen School. *Millennium* 29 (2): 285–306.

Hohmann, Jessie, and Daniel Joyce, eds. 2018. *International Law's Objects.* Cambridge: Cambridge University Press.

Johns, Fleur. 2013. *Non-Legality in International Law: Unruly Law.* Cambridge: Cambridge University Press.

Kendall, Sara, and Sarah Nouwen. 2013. Representational Practices at the International Criminal Court: The Gap between Juridified and Abstract Victimhood. *Law and Contemporary Problems* 76: 235–262.

Kennedy, David. 2018. *A World of Struggle: How Power, Law, and Expertise Shape Global Political Economy.* Princeton: Princeton University Press.

Koskenniemi, Martti. 1999. The Preamble of the Universal Declaration of Human Rights. In *The Universal Declaration of Human Rights: A Common Standard of Achievement*, ed. Gudmundur Alfredsson and Asbjørn Eide. Leiden: Martinus Nijhoff Publishers.

Koulen, Sarah-Jane. 2019. Blind Justice and the Portraits on the Wall. In *Illuminating the Backstage of Transnational Legal Practice*, ed. Lianne J.M. Boer and Sofia Stolk. London: Routledge.

Lisle, Debbie, and Heather Johnson. 2018. Lost in the Aftermath. *Security Dialogue* 50 (1): 20–39.

Madsen, Mikael. 2015. Sociological Approaches to International Courts. In *The Oxford Handbook of International Adjudication*, ed. Cesare Romano, Karen Alter, and Yuval Shany. Oxford: Oxford University Press.

Morgan, Edward M. 2007. *Aesthetics of International Law.* Toronto: University of Toronto Press.

Mowbray, Jacqueline. 2012. *Linguistic Justice: International Law and Language Policy.* Oxford: Oxford University Press.

Nouwen, Sarah. 2017. 'As You Set out for Ithaka: Practical, Epistemological, Ethical, and Existential Questions About Socio-Legal Empirical Research in Conflict. *Leiden Journal of International Law* 27: 227–260.

Nussbaum, Martha. 2013. *Political Emotions: Why Love Matters for Justice.* Cambridge: Belknap.

Odysseos, Louiza. 2017. Prolegomena to Any Future Decolonial Ethics: Coloniality, Poetics and 'Being Human as Praxis'. *Millennium* 45 (3): 447–472.

Orford, Anne, ed. 2009. *International Law and Its Others.* Cambridge: Cambridge University Press.

Otto, Dianne. 2017. Beyond Legal Justice: Some Personal Reflections on People's Tribunals, Listening and Responsibility. *London Review of International Law* 5 (2): 225–249.

Parfitt, Rose. 2017. The Anti-Neutral Suit: International Legal Futurists, 1914–2017. *London Review of International Law* 5 (1): 87–123.

———. 2019. *The Process of International Legal Reproduction: Inequality, Historiography, Resistance.* Cambridge: Cambridge University Press.

Parker, James. 2015. *Acoustic Jurisprudence: Listening to the Trial of Simon Bikindi.* Oxford: Oxford University Press.

Peters, Julie Stone. 2008. Legal Performance Good and Bad. *Law, Culture and the Humanities* 4: 179–200.

Rajkovic, Nikolas. 2019. Interdisciplinarity. In *Concepts for International Law*, ed. Jean d'Aspremont and Sahib Singh. Cheltenham: Edward Elgar.

Ranganathan, Surabhi. 2013. The Value of Narratives: The India-USA Nuclear Deal in Terms of Fragmentation, Pluralism, Constitutionalisation and Global Administrative Law. *Erasmus Law Review* 6 (17): 17–31.

Saugmann, Rune. 2019. Military Techno-Vision: Technologies Between Visual Ambiguity and the Desire for Security Facts. *European Journal of International Security* 4: 300–321.

Schweiger, Elisabeth. 2018. Listen Closely: What Silence Can Tell Us About Legal Knowledge Production. *London Review of International Law* 6 (3): 391: 411.

Schwöbel-Patel, Christine. 2013. The Comfort of International Criminal Law. *Law and Critique* 24 (2): 169–191.

———. 2018. The 'Ideal' Victim of International Criminal Law. *European Journal of International Law* 29 (3): 703–724.

Simpson, Gerry. 2015. The Sentimental Life of International Law. *London Review of International Law* 3 (1): 3–29.

Spivak, Gayatri. 1988. Can the Subaltern Speak? In *Marxism and the Interpretation of Culture*, ed. Cary Nelson and Lawrence Grossberg. Urbana, IL: University of Illinois Press.

Stolk, Sofia. 2015. "The Records on Which History Will Judge Us Tomorrow": Auto-History in the Opening Statements of International Criminal Trials. *Leiden Journal of International Law* 28 (4): 993–1012.

———. 2021, forthcoming. *The Opening Statement of the Prosecution in International Criminal Trials: A Solemn Tale of Horror.* London: Routledge.

Stolk, Sofia, and Renske Vos, eds. 2020a. Special Section: Brutal International Law: A Walk Through Marcel Breuer's Former American Embassy in The Hague. *New Perspectives* 28 (1): 12–70.

————. 2020b. International Legal Sightseeing. *Leiden Journal of International Law* 33 (1): 1–11.

Tallgren, Immi. 2017. Watching Tokyo Trial. *London Review of International Law* 5 (2): 291–316.

———— Stardust of Justice? Celebrity in and by International Law. Research Paper Prepared for the Law and Society Association Annual Meeting 2018, on File with Authors.

Tallis, Benjamin. 2019. Multiplicity: Taking Responsibility for The International. *New Perspectives* 27 (3): 166–173.

Tatar, Maria. 2003. *The Hard Facts of the Grimms' Fairy Tales*. Princeton: Princeton University Press.

Tranter, Kieran. 2017. Seeing Law: The Comic and Icon as Law. *International Journal for the Semiotics of Law/Revue Internationale de Sémiotique Juridique* 30 (3): 363–366.

Venzke, Ingo. 2012. *How Interpretation Makes International Law: On Semantic Change and Normative Twists*. Oxford: Oxford University Press.

Vos, Renske. 2020. *Europe and the Sea of Stories*. PhD Thesis, Vrije Universiteit, Amsterdam.

Warren, Christopher N. 2015. *Literature and the Law of Nations, 1580–1680*. Oxford: Oxford University Press.

Werner, Wouter. 2014. "We Cannot Allow Ourselves to Imagine What It All Means": Documentary Practices and the International Criminal Court. *Law and Contemporary Problems* 76: 319–340.

Werner, W.G. 2017. Recall It Again, Sam. Practices of Repetition in the Security Council. *Nordic Journal of International Law* 86 (2): 151–169.

White, James Boyd. 1985. *Heracles' Bow: Essays on the Rhetoric and Poetics of the Law*. Wisconsin: The University of Wisconsin Press.

Yahyaoui Krivenko, Ekatarina. 2015. International Law, Literature and Interdisciplinarity. *Law and Humanities* 9 (1): 103–122.

CHAPTER 2

Pride and Prejudice: Jane Austen and the (In)ability to Speak International Law

Elisabeth Schweiger and Aoife O'Leary McNeice

'Elizabeth made no answer, and, without attempting to persuade her ladyship to return to the house, walked quietly into it herself.'[1]

INTRODUCTION

Similar to international law, Jane Austen's novels have been critiqued for representing an orientalist, classist society, in which the main characters tend to be white and upper class, moving within a bubble of power and

---

[1] Jane Austen, *Pride and Prejudice* (Penguin: London, 1994, first pub. 1813), p. 276.

E. Schweiger (✉)
York University, York, UK
e-mail: elisabeth.schweiger@york.ac.uk

A. O'Leary McNeice
University of Cambridge, Cambridge, UK
e-mail: ao426@cam.ac.uk

© The Author(s), under exclusive license to Springer Nature Switzerland AG 2020
S. Stolk, R. Vos (eds.), *International Law's Collected Stories*, Palgrave Studies in International Relations, https://doi.org/10.1007/978-3-030-58835-9_2

17

privilege.[2] Marginalised actors are excluded from speaking and the elaborate power play of class, race and gender which propels the narrative is often left unmentioned. Jane Austen has received criticism, perhaps not least based on the shocking link between the quiet world of the narratives of 'gentle Jane' and the underlying horrors of colonialism, subjugation and slavery.[3] This is not unlike some critiques of international law, which are based on its construction as a romantic ideal. If international law is understood as an ordered, quiet, idealised world of principles, treaties and court judgements, the brutality of colonialism and power politics would be perceived as threatening international law—or rather calling into question a romanticised image of international law.

A closer look at Jane Austen's writing reveals an acute awareness of gendered and classed power relations encroaching into the ordered romance of the plot. These forces become visible in the implicit assumptions of characters, in moments when silence itself becomes audible. *Pride and Prejudice* is a story about who is allowed to speak and who is listened to. Building on the intricate constellation of relations of power between characters in the novel, this chapter highlights similar forms of exclusion within international law. The aim of the chapter is to open up analytical space to move beyond a romanticised ideal of international law by reading it through the power relations present in Jane Austen's work. Attempting to disrupt the conventional way of thinking of law, we use exclusion in *Pride and Prejudice* to draw attention to the politics of being (un)able to pronounce, to judge and speak international law.

We interrogate the ways in which communication in Jane Austen's *Pride and Prejudice* is embedded in power relations, in order to illustrate similar dynamics in international law. The chapter thus investigates contextual parameters which determine who has the agency to speak, what forms of communication are recognised and accepted, and how expectations might work to shape or overwrite the agency of the marginalised. *Pride and Prejudice* thus serves as a lens for us to reflect on the politics of international law and to recover the story of international law beyond a romanticised drawing room imagery.

---

[2] Edward Said, *Culture and Imperialism* (New York: Vintage Books, 1994), 80; G. E. Boulukos, "The Politics of Silence: Mansfield Park and the Amelioration of Slavery," *Novel: A Forum on Fiction* 39, no. 3 (June 1, 2006): 361–83.

[3] Susan Fraiman, "Jane Austen and Edward Said: Gender, Culture, and Imperialism," *Critical Inquiry* 21, no. 4 (1995): 809.

The Servants

As we shall discuss, many of the key plot points of *Pride and Prejudice* depend upon silence and mis-communication between key characters. However, there are far more silent figures in the novel than one might notice upon first glance. Indeed, there is a near constantly present cohort of largely silent servants that populate the periphery of the narrative. These people are only invoked when they can be of service to the plot, for example Mrs Nichols, the housekeeper of Longbourn, informs Mrs Philips of Bingley's return to Netherfield, saying the news was 'certainly true' because he had ordered a substantial amount of food from the butchers.[4] These servants represent a constantly present material reality of food and cleaning and also listening and transferring information. On one occasion Mr Bennet waits for the servants to leave before he assures his wife that Lydia and Wickham will never be welcome at Longbourn.[5] Yet, many of the servants do not appear as persons within the plot at all—and if they do, they cannot actively engage with the main characters, who move within a different sphere.

The story of international law tends to rely on similar mechanisms of exclusion. The ability to speak or gain a role in the plot is primarily based on the status of sovereign statehood. This silence has been formative for international law through its colonial legacy, determining state sovereignty as a process which (has) excluded the non-European world, not only from claiming certain rights of international law, but from having a legally recognisable voice in the first place.[6] The very way in which we tend to tell the story of international law is embedded in this legacy. Textbooks on international law will often recount it as a story of white, wealthy, European men. Time and time again—international law like a good tale lives from repetition—the story will start with 'once upon a time there was a man called Hugo Grotius'. Moving from one white, wealthy, European man to the next, the creation of principles such as state sovereignty is told to originate with a particular cast of characters.

Of course, stories also benefit from ideals of altruism and generosity. Indeed, one of the factors in Elizabeth's falling in love with Darcy is the positive report she receives about him from his long-time housekeeper at

---

[4] Austen, *Pride and Prejudice*, p. 254.
[5] Austen, *Pride and Prejudice*, p. 238.
[6] Antony Anghie, "Finding the Peripheries: Sovereignty and Colonialism in Nineteenth-Century International Law," *Harv. Int'l. LJ* 40 (1999): 3.

Pemberley, who assures her that 'I never had a cross word from him in my life, and I have known him ever since he was four years old.'[7] Yet, although her voice intrudes upon the text, the housekeeper remains a mere plot point, notable only due to her relation to Mr Darcy. Indeed, his silence is enabled by her speech, which reveals nothing about her other than her servitude to him. These power relations are quietly at work in a plot in which Mr Darcy is cast as the hero.

The story of international law is similarly told through the agency of European men, who are cast as having invented and then exported international law principles to the world. Skipping over the brutality underlying the formation and application of these principles, what is left is a story of agency by Western heroes, a story in which the feminised, non-elite, non-European world figures as the mute recipient of developments.[8] Erased are the multitudes of pioneering non-white, female, working-class people who pushed for principles, such as the Universal Declaration of Human Rights. Erased also are the struggles and political contestations by non-Western peoples through which state sovereignty became formally recognised as a universal principle against the direct interest of European imperialist elites.

We thus set up the story of international law in a very particular way. Similar to *Pride and Prejudice*, the plot is developed around a particular set of main characters while others are backgrounded, appearing exclusively in their relation to the main character and only when it is relevant for the plot. Unlike Jane Austen, we do not tend to recognise it as a fictional story. Yet, telling the story of international law in this way re-creates asymmetrical power relations and has repercussions for how agency is understood, how speech is interpreted and how new laws are developed.

THE PROPOSAL

Asymmetrical power relations can create a situation in which protest comes at a high cost. In *Pride and Prejudice*, when Elizabeth refuses her cousin, Mr Collins', proposal of marriage, her mother turns against her and

---

[7] Austen, *Pride and Prejudice*, p. 190.

[8] John M. Hobson, "Is Critical Theory Always for the White West and for Western Imperialism? Beyond Westphilian towards a Post-Racist Critical IR," *Review of International Studies* 33, no. S1 (April 2007): 91–116, https://doi.org/10.1017/S0260210507007413; Anghie, "Finding the Peripheries," 6.

punishes her. But even if a character is in a position to speak, this does not mean that their speech will be heard or will have any effect. Langton calls this 'illocutionary disablement', a situation in which a person might speak but the uttered words do not achieve the intended illocutionary act.[9] Exclusion in the novel *Pride and Prejudice* is not simply the absence of speech: some characters are silenced due to expectations around their gender, social status or the material circumstances of their lives and are rendered essentially mute despite their eloquence.

Such a silence is imposed upon Elizabeth when she rejects Mr Collins' proposal. Elizabeth's rejection of him is unequivocal; indeed, she interrupts him mid-speech: 'You are too hasty, sir...you forget that I have made no answer. Let me do it without further loss of time. Accept my thanks for the compliment you are paying me. I am very sensible of the honour of your proposals, but it is impossible for me to do otherwise than decline them.'[10] However, Mr Collins does not hear her words and instead treats her as a gendered archetype rather than an individual, assuring her that he is aware 'that it is usual with young ladies to reject the addresses of the man whom they secretly mean to accept.'[11] When Elizabeth continues to reject his advances he renders her speech meaningless by describing her refusal as 'merely words of course.'[12] He concludes that, based on her material circumstances, it is simply not conceivable that she can be serious, arguing that

> It does not appear to me that my hand is unworthy of your acceptance, or that the establishment I can offer would be any other than highly desirable. My situation in life, my connections with the family of de Bourgh, and my relationship to your own, are circumstances highly in my favour; and you should take into further consideration, that in spite of your manifold attractions, it is by no means certain that another offer of marriage may ever be made you. Your portion is unhappily so small, that it will in all likelihood, undo the effects of your loveliness and amiable qualifications. As I must therefore conclude that you are not serious in your rejection of me, I shall

---

[9] Rae Langton, "Speech Acts and Unspeakable Acts," *Philosophy & Public Affairs*, 1993, 315; see also Xavier Guillaume, "How to Do Things with Silence: Rethinking the Centrality of Speech to the Securitization Framework," *Security Dialogue*, 2018, 1–17.

[10] Austen, *Pride and Prejudice*, p. 86.

[11] Austen, *Pride and Prejudice*, p. 86.

[12] Austen, *Pride and Prejudice*, p. 86.

> chuse to attribute it to your wish of increasing my love by suspense, accord-
> ing to the usual practice of elegant females[13]

Due to her gender and material circumstances, Mr Collins is unable to conceive of Elizabeth as an individual who does not adhere to the conventions of society despite her clear articulation of her desires. Indeed, Elizabeth herself identifies this, pleading with him, 'do not consider me now as an elegant female, intending to plague you, but as a rational creature, speaking the truth from her heart.'[14] She bristles under his reduction of her to a type and his denial of her voice. Elizabeth's position in society means that her speech is rendered silent by those who identify her based solely on her gender and the material circumstances of her life.

In international law, silence has also operated as acquiescence to the detriment of those who are not configured as speaking subjects. In the justification of colonial violence, such as for the acquisition of *terra nullius* (land which was considered ownerless), acquiescence thus played an important role. Protest required sovereign statehood and excluded non-European voices from speaking in a legally meaningful way.[15] In a circular move, this non-objection then served to legitimate the acquisition since it confirmed 'the likelihood that the territory was *terra nullius* at the critical date'.[16]

Yet 'illocutionary disablement' depends not only on formal recognition of subjecthood but on a wide network of power relations. For the formation, pronouncement and interpretation of international law, silencing dynamics within legal knowledge production play a key role in the politics of what is included or excluded. This means the exclusion of non-state voices but also the rendering irrelevant (or not mentioning) of certain state voices. When, for example, the Colombian government killed suspected FARC fighters in Ecuador in 2008, Latin American states clearly positioned themselves in opposition to this use of force. The Venezuelan government mobilised tank battalions to the border with Colombia in

---

[13] Austen, *Pride and Prejudice*, pp. 87–88.

[14] Austen, *Pride and Prejudice*, p. 88

[15] Anghie, "Finding the Peripheries".

[16] I. C. MacGibbon, "Scope of Acquiescence in International Law, The," *British Year Book of International Law* 31 (1954): 143.

protest[17] and the Organization of American States objected to the intervention, calling it 'a violation of the sovereignty and territorial integrity of Ecuador'.[18] This protest of the most affected countries around Latin America is discounted when an overall conclusion is made 'that the international community—with the exception of Latin American states—tacitly accepted Colombia's expansive interpretation of the right to self-defence'[19] and that 'none of the principal organisations of the United Nations criticized the action'.[20] Like Mr Collins, we sometimes do not hear objections even when they are made by actors formally recognised as speaking subjects.

Silencing dynamics within legal knowledge can be based on banal methodological reasons.[21] Statements of governments appear and disappear in newspapers, websites, platforms of international organisations, scholarship and so on. The predominantly anglophone field of International Law often depends heavily on Western media outlets and sources available in English.[22] This influences which statements are heard at all within legal expertise. The methodological focus on Western sources influences which issues are taken notice of (or not) in legal discourses and which actors are heard.

[17] Tatiana Waisberg, "The Colombia–Ecuador Armed Crisis of March 2008: The Practice of Targeted Killing and Incursions against Non-State Actors Harbored at Terrorist Safe Havens in a Third Party State," *Studies In Conflict & Terrorism* 32, no. 6 (2009): 478.

[18] Organization of American States, "CP/RES. 930 (1632/08) Convocation of the Meeting of Consultation of Ministers of Foreign Affairs and Appointment of a Commission," 2008, https://www.oas.org/council/resolutions/res930.asp.

[19] Theresa Reinold, "State Weakness, Irregular Warfare, and the Right to Self-Defense Post-9/11," *The American Journal of International Law* 105, no. 2 (April 1, 2011): 274, https://doi.org/10.5305/amerjintelaw.105.2.0244.

[20] Kenneth Anderson, "Targeted Killing in U.S. Counterterrorism Strategy and Law," SSRN Scholarly Paper (Rochester, NY: Social Science Research Network, May 11, 2009), 20, http://papers.ssrn.com/abstract=1415070.

[21] see for further discussion Elisabeth Schweiger, "Listen Closely: What Silence Can Tell Us about Legal Knowledge Production," *London Review of International Law* 6, no. 3 (2018): 391–411.

[22] J. Patrick Kelly, "The Twilight of Customary International Law," *Va. J. Int'l L.* 40 (1999): 472; B. S. Chimni, "Customary International Law: A Third World Perspective," *American Journal of International Law* 112, no. 1 (January 2018): 1–46, https://doi.org/10.1017/ajil.2018.12.

MR AND MRS BENNETT

Many of the most crucial plot points of Jane Austen's *Pride and Prejudice* are shrouded in silence, whether it is Mr Darcy reluctantly falling in love with Elizabeth while watching her across a crowded ballroom, the silent communication of letter writing, or the deep feelings transferred between Jane and Elizabeth with just a smile or a meaningful gaze. However, speech and silence cannot be cordoned off from one another so neatly in the novel. The loudest characters in the novel are often the most foolish and deceitful, be it Mr Collins' silly incantations of Fordyce's sermons, the garish gossip of Mrs Bennet, or the misleading gregarious charm of Mr Wickham.

Silence is used as a weapon by Mr Bennet in the very first interaction in the novel. His wife requests that he call upon Mr Bingley, so that she and her daughters may then meet the eligible young wealthy man. She exclaims with her characteristic bombast, 'a single man of large fortune....What a fine thing for our girls!'[23] Mr Bennet in turn responds with characteristic belligerence, feigning ignorance and asking how Mr Bingley's position can affect their daughters, to which his wife responds with exasperation that she is 'thinking of him marrying one of them'.[24] This abrasive exchange between Mr Bennet, who communicates mostly with silence, and Mrs Bennet, who is one of the most talkative characters in the novel, reveals the power struggle which defines their marriage. Mrs Bennet is constantly and acutely aware of the fact that their home, Longbourn, is entailed, and upon the death of her husband, she and her daughters will likely be evicted by the closest male heir to her husband. Her unending talk of marriages is thus not simply idle chatter, but her attempt to achieve financial stability for herself and her daughters.

However, she is at the mercy of her husband, as social conventions dictate that she cannot call upon or communicate with Mr Bingley without the head of her household doing so first. Mr Bennet does in fact call on Mr Bingley quite promptly, yet he conceals this information from his wife and daughters for as long as possible. He deliberately provokes his wife by bringing up the subject of Mr Bingley before revealing to her that he has already visited him. It is a comedic exchange, but also one in which the power dynamic of their marriage is laid bare. Although she speaks more

---

[23] Austen, *Pride and Prejudice*, p. 5.
[24] Austen, *Pride and Prejudice*, p. 5.

than her husband, Mrs Bennet is rendered silent by his silence, as he prevents her from communicating with Mr Bingley by pretending to neglect his role as interlocutor. He uses his silence to demonstrate the power he wields over his wife, a power predicated by established gender norms.

Speech and silence are not binaries. Some characters might speak more but not be listened to and others are noted through their silence. As an act of communication, silence is deeply linked to wider forms of marginalisation. Feminist and post-colonial scholars have investigated such dynamics in the international realm.[25] Enloe, for example, speaks of 'the actual amount and the amazing variety of power that are required to keep the voices on the margins from having the right language and enough volume to be heard'.[26] Silence as a form of exclusion has been called 'silencing', defined as the process through which voices, issues and forms of speaking are excluded from certain discourses.[27] Silence here manifests itself not only in the exclusion of subaltern voices from hegemonic discourse, but in the way in which the very existence of differences is denied, and the language through which alternative experiences could be transmitted is constructed as unintelligible.[28] As the example of Mr and Mrs Bennett shows, this need not necessarily take place through an actual absence of words. The silencing of voices can operate by restricting access to discourses, or by belittling, ridiculing, not taking seriously—in short not hearing—particular utterances.[29]

[25] Kennan Ferguson, "Silence: A Politics," *Contemporary Political Theory* 2, no. 1 (March 2003): 52; J. Maggio, "'Can the Subaltern Be Heard?': Political Theory, Translation, Representation, and Gayatri Chakravorty Spivak," *Alternatives: Global, Local, Political* 32, no. 4 (October 2007): 419–43; Anne Orford, "Feminism, Imperialism and the Mission of International Law," *Nordic Journal of International Law* 71, no. 2 (2002): 275–296; Sophia Dingli, "We Need to Talk about Silence: Re-Examining Silence in International Relations Theory," *European Journal of International Relations* 21, no. 4 (2015): 1354066114568033.

[26] Cynthia H. Enloe, *The Curious Feminist: Searching for Women in a New Age of Empire* (Berkeley: University of California Press, 2004), 23; see also Orford, "Feminism, Imperialism and the Mission of International Law," 279.

[27] Lynn Janet Thiesmeyer, *Discourse and Silencing. Representation and the Language of Displacement*, 2003.

[28] Dingli, "We Need to Talk about Silence"; Anghie, "Finding the Peripheries".

[29] Lisa Block De Behar, *A Rhetoric of Silence and Other Selected Writings*, vol. 122 (Walter de Gruyter, 1995).

These dynamics are crucial for international law because 'in international law, naming is what produces knowledge';[30] how treaties come about, how international law is interpreted, how law is pronounced and judged upon, all depends on the ability to speak and be heard. In much scholarship of international law, this ability is taken for granted. States, as the law-givers in international law, are presumed able to speak. As one international law scholar put it: 'The argument sometimes raised that the omission of any protest may be due to a reason other than the tacit acceptance of the practice is unconvincing. Whatever the reason for such an omission, nowadays a State does this at its own risk'.[31] This inscription of silence onto international law tends to overlook complex dynamics of silencing and exclusion—of how voice is gained and silence becomes communicative.

Mr Darcy

Unlike Mrs Bennet, Mr Darcy is a character whose perceived social standing and power enables not just his speech, but his silence to be heard—and to be heard louder than the speech of others. Throughout the novel, rather than causing him to be ignored or erased from the narrative, Mr Darcy's silence is minutely described, interrogated and analysed by the narrator and the other characters in the novel. It speaks to the complexity of his inner thoughts, or his prejudice, or his social anxiety. For example, much is made of Mr Darcy's silence at the first ball he attends. During their post-mortem of the event, Charlotte, Mrs Bingley, Jane and Elizabeth devote much time to his silence. Mrs Bennet expresses her disdain for him: 'he is such a disagreeable man…it would be quite a misfortune to be liked by him. Mrs Long told me last night that he sat close to her for half-an-hour without once opening his lips'.[32] Jane takes a more charitable approach, in a manner which reflects her own character, which is generous and open hearted almost to a fault, reporting that Miss Bingley told her 'that he never speaks much unless among his intimate acquaintance. With

---

[30] Jean D'Aspremont, "Wording in International Law," *Leiden Journal of International Law* 25, no. 3 (September 2012): 582.

[31] K. Wolfke, "Some Persistent Controversies Regarding Customary International Law," *Netherlands Yearbook of International Law* 24 (December 1993): 9.

[32] Austen, *Pride and Prejudice*, p. 17.

them he is remarkably agreeable'.[33] The conversation continues, with each woman expressing her opinion of Darcy and his silence.

The scene reveals more about the nature of the women themselves than about Mr Darcy, and Jane even unknowingly alludes to Miss Bingley's jealous courtship of Darcy. The scene serves to reveal the power of Mr Darcy, due to his wealth and social standing; even his lack of engagement is treated with a great deal of attention. Indeed, even the narrator treats Darcy's silence with voyeuristic detail, describing how, when Elizabeth arrived at Netherfield after her walk from Longbourn, 'Mr Darcy said very little, and Mr Hurst nothing at all. The former was divided between admiration of the brilliancy which exercise had given to her complexion, and doubt as to the occasions justifying her coming so far alone. The latter was thinking only of his breakfast'.[34] This extract displays Austen's characteristic wit, but it also signposts the significance of Darcy's silence. There are also moments when his silence is invoked as censure. For example, whilst staying at Rosings, Lady Catherine de Bourgh rudely chides Elizabeth for not taking her up on the offer of practising music on the pianoforte in her house. Austen writes that 'Mr Darcy looked a little ashamed of his aunt's ill-breeding, and made no answer'.[35]

For international law, similar dynamics can be observed. There is often a focus on the practices and justifications of a minority of powerful states. Concentrating on the loud voices and contentious claims of powerful actors, however, ends up reinforcing these claims and backgrounding other perspectives.[36] In the legal debates on the invasion of Yugoslavia, for example, the practices by NATO states were emphasised while 'the reticence and protest of other [non-NATO] states (such as members of the non-aligned movement), on the other hand, were minimized; ignored, even'.[37]

The focus on more powerful actors ensures that not just their speech but also their silences gain a prominent role in the plot. Recently, there

---

[33] Austen, *Pride and Prejudice*, p. 17.
[34] Austen, *Pride and Prejudice*, p. 35.
[35] Austen, *Pride and Prejudice*, p. 136.
[36] Hilary Charlesworth, "International Law: A Discipline of Crisis," *Modern Law Review* 65, no. 3 (May 2002): 377–92; Olivier Corten, "The Controversies over the Customary Prohibition on the Use of Force: A Methodological Debate," *European Journal of International Law* 16, no. 5 (2005): 803–822.
[37] Corten, "The Controversies over the Customary Prohibition on the Use of Force," 811; see for a similar argument Christine Gray, *International Law and the Use of Force*, 2008, 117.

have been heated debates on a more expansive interpretation of the right to self-defence in counterterrorism use of force, where particularly the silence of European states has received a great deal of attention.[38] Similar to Mr Darcy's silence, the silence of European states has been discussed in policy discourses and international law literature, speculating as to what it might mean and its consequences for international law.[39] There is an assumption of subjecthood underlying the importance which some characters' silences receive, which backgrounds the silences and utterances by other characters and reaffirms the power of the figure of 'Mr Darcy'.

LADY DE BOURGH

The language determined by dominant discourses sets up parameters of the script in a particular way. Staying within this language game means accepting the rules set by it. It is in this context that silence can also function as a powerful move of subversion and resistance.[40] Indeed, in contrast to the engagement scene in which Elizabeth's constant protestations are silenced, her silence and refusal to engage in the language of polite discourse with Lady Catherine de Bourgh are a powerful and effective bulwark against the hierarchies of class and economics, which situate the latter far above the former.

Throughout the novel, Lady de Bourgh uses speech to enforce her power over others, be it her interior design suggestions, her strenuous recommendation that Elizabeth practise on the pianoforte, or her attempts to interfere with Elizabeth's travel plans. Indeed, during her final interaction with Elizabeth she addresses this, saying 'my character has ever been

---

[38] See, for example, Avery Plaw and Joao Franco Reis, "The Contemporary Practice of Self-Defense: Evolving Toward the Use of Preemptive or Preventive Force?," in *Preventive Force: Drones, Targeted Killing, and the Transformation of Contemporary Warfare*, ed. Kerstin Fisk and Jennifer M. Ramos, 2016.

[39] ICCT, "Towards a European Position on the Use of Armed Drones; International Centre for Counter-Terrorism, The Hague," 2016; Nathalie Van Raemdonck, *Vested Interest Or Moral Indecisiveness?: Explaining the EU's Silence on the US Targeted Killing Policy in Pakistan* (Istituto affari internazionali, 2012); Anthony Dworkin, "Drones and Targeted Killing: Defining a European Position," 2013.

[40] Xavier Guillaume and Elisabeth Schweiger, "Silence as Doing," in *Political Silence: Meanings, Functions and Ambiguity*, ed. Sophia Dingli and Thomas Cooke, 1st ed. (London: Routledge, 2018); Margaret E. Montoya, "Silence and Silencing: Their Centripetal and Centrifugal Forces in Legal Communication, Pedagogy and Discourse," *U. Mich. JL Reform* 33 (1999): 263.

celebrated for its sincerity and frankness, and in a cause of such moment as this I shall certainly not depart from it'.[41] This interaction is made all the more complicated by the fact that the information that has brought Lady de Bourgh to Longbourn—a rumour that Mr Darcy and Elizabeth are engaged—is false. However, Lady de Bourgh's act of travelling to Longbourn to break up the engagement ultimately ensures that it will take place, as Elizabeth's response to her convinces Mr Darcy that she is in love with him. Moreover, as Elizabeth points out, such an act, rather than dispelling rumours of the engagement, in fact seems to confirm them: she says to Lady de Bourgh 'your coming to Longbourn, to see me and my family...will be rather a confirmation of it; if indeed, such a report is in existence'.[42]

This interaction reveals the intersection of mis-information, rumour and action. The raw nature of the interaction is due to the fact that the conventions of polite conversation are stripped away. Elizabeth refuses to practice the polite silence to which Lady Catherine is accustomed, but also wards off her direct questions, refusing to answer directly and calling upon silence as a defence mechanism. Lady de Bourgh presses Elizabeth to confirm that there is no truth in the rumours of her engagement to Mr Darcy, but Elizabeth further increases the existing ambiguity and responds, 'I do not pretend to possess equal frankness with your ladyship. *You* may ask questions, which *I* shall not chuse to answer'.[43]

Silence can be a form of resistance within a discourse to 'discomfit those who regulate social behaviour with speech'.[44] Investigating silences in interviews, Clayman and Clayman have pointed to the strong social norm of speaking and how silence can function to disregard certain claims, prompts or speakers, demonstrating that it is not relevant or unworthy of response.[45] This can be communicated by explicitly framing silence. Hence, for example, the silence of the representative of the United Arab Emirates in a Security Council debate on the US bombing of Libya: 'I

[41] Austen, *Pride and Prejudice*, p. 272.
[42] Austen, *Pride and Prejudice*, p. 272.
[43] Austen, *Pride and Prejudice*, p. 273.
[44] Ferguson, "Silence," 56.
[45] Steven E. Clayman "Answers and Evasions," *Language in Society* 30, no. 3 (September 1, 2001): 422.

would have preferred to speak at greater length and to answer the arguments and evidence adduced, if there had been any point in doing so'.[46]

The important role silence can play for those in a less powerful position is often overlooked in international law—even though it is ultimately through silence that the boundaries of international law become defined. Investigating the process through which issues gain discursive existence, Bourdieu has pointed to the importance of whether something is translated into legal language, thus becoming an object of juridical debate.[47] Silence can work to denote the irrelevance of an issue in a discourse. It is this function of silence which Koskenniemi refers to in the context of the International Court of Justice's silence regarding the decision on the legality of nuclear weapons. He argues that translating the question into juridical language would have lifted the matter 'onto the level of judicial reason' and the silence of the Court avoided this.[48]

In complex political and social circumstances, silence can be an important discursive move for those unable to alter the script. Jane Austen reveals the rich tapestry silence is embedded in, far beyond a mere question of acquiescence. In *Pride and Prejudice*, silence is explicitly invoked in over 160 instances, not only as deferral but to showcase moments of disrespect,[49] or how things cannot be said for diplomatic reasons, when 'the delicacy of it prevented farther inquiry'.[50] Particularly the show-down between Elizabeth and Lady de Bourgh at the end of the novel reveals the subversive potential of silence.

Lady de Bourgh continues to grill Elizabeth without receiving her desired response, prompting her to directly refer to her social standing and the manner in which she is usually addressed: 'Miss Bennet, do you know who I am? I have not been accustomed to such language as this'.[51] This direct reference to terms of conversational engagement is rare in a novel characterised by linguistic subtleties and meaningful glances. In this

---

[46] UN Doc S/PV.2674, "United Nations Security Council Debate (2674th Meeting)," 1986, 4.

[47] Pierre Bourdieu, "Force of Law: Toward a Sociology of the Juridical Field," *Hastings LJ* 38 (1986): 835.

[48] Martti Koskenniemi, "The Silence of Law," in *International Law, the International Court of Justice and Nuclear Weapons* (Cambridge: Boisson de Chazournes and Sands, 1999), 496.

[49] Austen, *Pride and Prejudice*, pp. 168, 179.

[50] Austen, *Pride and Prejudice*, p. 79.

[51] Austen, *Pride and Prejudice*, p. 273.

moment the weaponised nature of language is laid bare. Discourse is stripped of its polite niceties as these two characters battle for discursive supremacy. The role that silence and listening play in this exchange is highlighted in one particular moment of dialogue, when Lady de Bourgh invites Elizabeth to sit:

> 'Let us sit down. You are to understand, Miss Bennet, that I came here with the determined resolution of carrying my purpose; nor will I be dissuaded from it. I have not been used to submit to any person's whims. I have not been in the habit of brooking disappointment.'
>
> '*That* will make your ladyship's situation at present more pitiable; but it will have no effect on *me.*'
>
> 'I will not be interrupted! Hear me in silence. My daughter and my nephew are formed for each other. They are descended on the maternal side, from the same noble line; and, on their fathers', from respectable, honourable, and ancient, though untitled families. Their fortune on both sides is splendid. They are destined for each other by the voice of every member of their respective houses; and what is to divide them? The upstart pretensions of a young woman without family, connections, or fortune. Is this to be endured? But it must not, shall not be! If you were sensible of your own good, you would not wish to quit the sphere in which you have been brought up.'
>
> 'In marrying your nephew I should not consider myself as quitting that sphere. He is a gentleman; I am a gentleman's daughter: so far we are equal.'
>
> 'True. You *are* a gentleman's daughter. But who was your mother? Who are your uncles and aunts? Do not imagine me ignorant of their condition.'[52]

In this exchange the social tensions that ordinarily bubble under the surface of the novel's dialogue are laid bare, meaningful glances and disdainful silences become vocalised invocations of class snobbery and the affirmation of social hierarchy. Lady de Bourgh silences Elizabeth by departing from polite conversation and openly critiquing her upbringing and social position. Elizabeth has forced her to do so by her refusal to adhere to these social hierarchies, and denying Lady de Bourgh the answer she desires.

The power this subversion of social niceties gives Elizabeth is affirmed as the end of the exchange draws near, and she essentially dismisses Lady de Bourgh, 'Lady Catherine, I have nothing further to say. You know my

---

[52] Austen, *Pride and Prejudice*, p. 274.

sentiments'.[53] When leaving, Lady de Bourgh expresses her anger by expressly flouting polite conventions, 'I take no leave of you, Miss Bennet. I send no compliments to your mother. You deserve no such attention. I am seriously displeased'.[54] In a final display of power, Elizabeth replies with silence: 'Elizabeth made no answer, and, without attempting to persuade her ladyship to return to the house, walked quietly into it herself'.[55] This is the dramatic dénouement of the novel: a story defined by silence and the minutiae of polite conversation climaxes in a raw conflict in which the crudities of the social hierarchies within which the novel's characters are forced to inhabit are laid bare.

CONCLUSION

In her celebrated extended essay *A Room of One's Own*, published in 1929, Virginia Woolf described how 'masculine values prevail' when judging the importance or otherwise of a piece of literature.[56] She wrote, 'this is an important book, the critic assumes, because it deals with war. This is an insignificant book because it deals with the feelings of women in a drawing-room. A scene in a battle-field is more important than a scene in a shop—everywhere and much more subtly the difference of value persists'.[57] This essay seeks to redress this disparity. *Pride and Prejudice* may not immediately strike one as a novel that lends itself to interpretations of international law and conflicts between global actors, yet the dynamics Austen creates between her characters are universal, be they wielded by powerful individuals or powerful nations over the weak or subaltern.

Approaching international law through Jane Austen's *Pride and Prejudice*, this chapter has examined forms of exclusion from speaking international law. Moving beyond a binary understanding of silence and speech, we built on the intricate power relations in Jane Austen's work which show how deeply linked the question of silence is to implicit assumptions about subjectivities of speakers and their agency. While some actors' speech is attentively listened to, others' speech becomes mere background chatter. The dominant scripts shape particular forms of communication

---

[53] Austen, *Pride and Prejudice*, p. 276.

[54] Austen, *Pride and Prejudice*, p. 276.

[55] Austen, *Pride and Prejudice*, p. 276.

[56] Virginia Woolf, *A Room of One's Own* (London: Hogarth Press, 1931, first pub., 1929), p. 111.

[57] Woolf, *A Room of One's Own*, p. 111.

and set the parameters of communication up in ways that privileges the speech—and silence—of some actors and erases other characters from the plot.

While international law often perceives speech and silence as linked to the simplified assumption of agency through the subjectivity of sovereign statehood, *Pride and Prejudice* reveals how silence is embedded within complex power relations. This is not just a question of material power and status but is deeply engrained in the listeners' expectations of what can and should be said and in what way.

BIBLIOGRAPHY

Anderson, Kenneth. Targeted Killing in U.S. Counterterrorism Strategy and Law. SSRN Scholarly Paper. Rochester, NY: Social Science Research Network, May 11, 2009. http://papers.ssrn.com/abstract=1415070.

Anghie, Antony. 1999. Finding the Peripheries: Sovereignty and Colonialism in Nineteenth-Century International Law. *Harvard International Law Journal* 40: 1.

Austen, Jane Pride and Prejudice, London (1994, First Pub. 1813).

Boulukos, G.E. 2006. The Politics of Silence: Mansfield Park and the Amelioration of Slavery. *Novel: A Forum on Fiction* 39 (3): 361–383. https://doi.org/10.1215/ddnov.039030361.

Bourdieu, Pierre. 1986. Force of Law: Toward a Sociology of the Juridical Field. *The Hastings Law Journal* 38: 805.

Charlesworth, Hilary. 2002. International Law: A Discipline of Crisis. *Modern Law Review* 65 (3): 377–392.

Chimni, B.S. 2018. Customary International Law: A Third World Perspective. *American Journal of International Law* 112 (1): 1–46. https://doi.org/10.1017/ajil.2018.12.

Clayman, Steven E., and Steve E. Clayman. 2001. Answers and Evasions. *Language in Society* 30 (3): 403–442.

Corten, Olivier. 2005. The Controversies Over the Customary Prohibition on the Use of Force: A Methodological Debate. *European Journal of International Law* 16 (5): 803–822.

D'Aspremont, Jean. 2012. Wording in International Law. *Leiden Journal of International Law* 25 (3): 575–602.

De Behar, Lisa Block. 1995. *A Rhetoric of Silence and Other Selected Writings*. Vol. 122. Walter de Gruyter.

Dingli, Sophia. 2015. We Need to Talk About Silence: Re-Examining Silence in International Relations Theory. *European Journal of International Relations* 21 (4): 1354066114568033.

Dworkin, Anthony. 2013. Drones and Targeted Killing: Defining a European Position.

Enloe, Cynthia H. 2004. *The Curious Feminist: Searching for Women in a New Age of Empire*. Berkeley: University of California Press.

Ferguson, Kennan. 2003. Silence: A Politics. *Contemporary Political Theory* 2 (1): 49.

Fraiman, Susan. 1995. Jane Austen and Edward Said: Gender, Culture, and Imperialism. *Critical Inquiry* 21 (4): 805–821.

Gray, Christine. 2008. *International Law and the Use of Force*. Routledge.

Guillaume, Xavier. 2018. How to Do Things with Silence: Rethinking the Centrality of Speech to the Securitization Framework. *Security Dialogue*: 1–17.

Guillaume, Xavier, and Elisabeth Schweiger. 2018. Silence as Doing. In *Political Silence: Meanings, Functions and Ambiguity*, ed. Sophia Dingli and Thomas Cooke, 1st ed. London: Routledge.

Hobson, John M. 2007. Is Critical Theory Always for the White West and for Western Imperialism? Beyond Westphilian Towards a Post-Racist Critical IR. *Review of International Studies* 33 (S1): 91–116. https://doi.org/10.1017/S0260210507007413.

ICCT. 2016. *Towards a European Position on the Use of Armed Drones*. The Hague: International Centre for Counter-Terrorism.

Kelly, J.Patrick. 1999. The Twilight of Customary International Law. *Virginia Journal of International Law* 40: 449.

Koskenniemi, Martti. 1999. The Silence of Law. In *International Law, the International Court of Justice and Nuclear Weapons*. Cambridge: Boisson de Chazournes and Sands.

Langton, Rae. 1993. Speech Acts and Unspeakable Acts. *Philosophy & Public Affairs*: 293–330.

MacGibbon, I.C. 1954. Scope of Acquiescence in International Law, The. *British Year Book of International Law* 31: 143.

Maggio, J. 2007. 'Can the Subaltern Be Heard?': Political Theory, Translation, Representation, and Gayatri Chakravorty Spivak. *Alternatives: Global, Local, Political* 32 (4): 419–443.

Montoya, Margaret E. 1999. Silence and Silencing: Their Centripetal and Centrifugal Forces in Legal Communication, Pedagogy and Discourse. *University of Michigan Journal of Law Reform* 33: 263.

Orford, Anne. 2002. Feminism, Imperialism and the Mission of International Law. *Nordic Journal of International Law* 71 (2): 275–296.

Organization of American States. CP/RES. 930 (1632/08) Convocation of the Meeting of Consultation of Ministers of Foreign Affairs and Appointment of a Commission, 2008. https://www.oas.org/council/resolutions/res930.asp.

Plaw, Avery, and Joao Franco Reis. 2016. The Contemporary Practice of Self-Defense: Evolving Toward the Use of Preemptive or Preventive Force? In *Preventive Force: Drones, Targeted Killing, and the Transformation of Contemporary Warfare*, ed. Kerstin Fisk and Jennifer M. Ramos. New York: New York University Press.

Reinold, Theresa. 2011. State Weakness, Irregular Warfare, and the Right to Self-Defense Post-9/11. *The American Journal of International Law* 105 (2): 244–286. https://doi.org/10.5305/amerjintelaw.105.2.0244.

Said, Edward. 1994. *Culture and Imperialism*. New York: Vintage Books.

Schweiger, Elisabeth. 2018. Listen Closely: What Silence Can Tell Us about Legal Knowledge Production. *London Review of International Law* 6 (3): 391–411.

Thiesmeyer, Lynn Janet. 2003. *Discourse and Silencing. Representation and the Language of Displacement*. Amsterdam: J. Benjamins.

UN Doc S/PV.2674. United Nations Security Council Debate (2674th Meeting), 1986.

Van Raemdonck, Nathalie. 2012. *Vested Interest Or Moral Indecisiveness?: Explaining the EU's Silence on the US Targeted Killing Policy in Pakistan*. Istituto affari internazionali.

Waisberg, Tatiana. 2009. The Colombia–Ecuador Armed Crisis of March 2008: The Practice of Targeted Killing and Incursions Against Non-State Actors Harbored at Terrorist Safe Havens in a Third Party State. *Studies in Conflict & Terrorism* 32 (6): 476–488.

Wolfke, K. 1993. Some Persistent Controversies Regarding Customary International Law. *Netherlands Yearbook of International Law* 24: 1–16. https://doi.org/10.1017/S0167676800000027.

Woolf, Virginia. (1931, first pub., 1929). *A Room of One's Own*, London: Hogarth Press.

CHAPTER 3

Staging International Law's Stories: *Kapo in Jerusalem*

Mark Drumbl

How to speak of victims who victimize others? Of the pain they cause? Of the memories that result? Of what it means to persecute while suffering persecution? This chapter unpacks how the stage—theatrical, taut, and thespian—refracts these questions. It does so through one of the most invidious blights of the Holocaust, that is, the SS policy to coerce and enlist detainees into the administration of Nazi labor and death camps. The SS established a number of categories in this odious hierarchy of 'prisoner self-administration'. Among these categories were the Kapos: detainees, including Jewish detainees, who supervised forced laborers by day and lorded over the barracks by night.[1]

Kapos constitute a particularly contested element of Holocaust remembrance. Some Kapos deployed their situational authority to ease the

---

[1] Michael Marrus, *The Holocaust in History* (New York: Penguin, 1987), 129 (describing the Kapo: 'The Nazis … empowered camp elders, clerks, block leaders, and so forth to supervise the inmates and assume primary responsibility for the routines of daily life').

M. Drumbl (✉)
Washington and Lee University, Lexington, VA, USA
e-mail: DrumblM@wlu.edu

© The Author(s), under exclusive license to Springer Nature
Switzerland AG 2020
S. Stolk, R. Vos (eds.), *International Law's Collected Stories*,
Palgrave Studies in International Relations,
https://doi.org/10.1007/978-3-030-58835-9_3

conditions of other prisoners, while others acted cruelly and committed abuses. While many Kapos were compelled to serve, others made their services available—at times readily—so as to prolong their lives or the lives of their families. Kapos were organized in pyramidal fashion. More influential Kapos included the *Blockälteste* (mid-level, barracks 'elder') going up to the chief Kapo. While still tenuously positioned, and always occupying liminal spaces,[2] more senior Kapos exercised considerable situational authority. Referencing all Kapos, Primo Levi noted that 'the power of these small satraps was absolute'.[3]

This chapter interrogates one presentation of the Kapo, namely, the stage play *Kapo Be'Yerushalaim* (*Kapo in Jerusalem*) (2014) written by Motti Lerner in Hebrew and translated into English by Roy Isacowitz.[4] This chapter stages the play, so to speak, so that stories ferment in the minds of readers. This play adapts and is derivative of a film of the same title directed by Uri Barbash and produced by Haim Sharir in 2014 (98 minutes in length).

The stage play (and film) is rooted around an atrocity trial in the guise of an administrative proceeding (the expulsion of a physician collaborator from the Israeli medical association)—a dream of sorts—that evokes themes central to the construction of the state of Israel and the sutures of international law. Camp survivors appear disembodied as attorney-witnesses. One group condemns while the other group justifies. In between there is no 'truth'. Although the stage play is fictional, it (along with the film) is inspired by a Kapo named Eliezer Gruenbaum. Born in Poland in 1908, Gruenbaum was 'a brilliant and attractive young man, a

---

[2] Adam Brown, *Judging "Privileged" Jews: Holocaust Ethics, Representation and the "Grey Zone"* (Oxford: Berghahn, 2015), 12: '*Kapos* were subject to punishment by Nazi guards for any problems arising from the prisoners they were responsible for [...]'.

[3] Primo Levi, *The Drowned and the Saved*, trans. Raymond Rosenthal (London: Michael Joseph, 1st ed. 1988), 31.

[4] The full text of the play is available for open and free public access at the Israeli Dramatists Website, 'Kapo in Jerusalem', Drama Israel, visited: January 15, 2019, http://dramaisrael. org/wp-content/uploads/2014/12/Kapo-in-Jerusalem-September-2014.pdf (noting specifically copyright of the author and that 'All dramatic rights in this play are fully protected by copyright and no public or private performance—professional or amateur—and no public readings for profit may be given without the written permission of the author and the payment of royalty. Communications should be addressed to the Author's representative: Susan Schulman A Literary Agency, 454 West 44th St. New York, New York 10036 T: (212) 713–1633 F: (212) 581–8830'). Scholarly discussion of this play within this chapter falls outside of these protected grounds and, furthermore, we maintain it is subject to the fair dealing doctrine.

gifted speaker, and at the same time hot-tempered and stubborn'.[5] He became a prisoner and deputy *blockführer* in Auschwitz-Birkenau in charge of 900 prisoners. Gruenbaum emigrated to Israel in 1946 and died in a battle in Israel's War of Independence in 1948. Gruenbaum left detailed memoirs, which were published in 1952. The stage play nests and is rooted in these memoirs, which Gruenbaum titled 'In the Courtyards of Death'. While a 'statement of defense' of sorts, and an *apologia* of the 'moral code' Gruenbaun developed in a world of depravity and abject immorality, these memoirs also serve to plunge the reader into the toxicity of Auschwitz.[6]

This chapter interrogates how the play *Kapo in Jerusalem* expresses the stories, experiences, navigations, and tactics of victims who hurt others. Telling the story that this play tells—a very powerful one, forcefully narrated, of law, judgment, suicide, shame, and the deployment of violence to supposedly protect others—serves as a kind of 'picture book' of the potential and limits of international law.

While summarizing the play, and thereby staging it for the reader, this chapter also on occasion didactically gestures toward themes of responsibility, truth, justice, and punishment that redound upon and preoccupy law. This chapter is a companion to, and entwines with, three other projects: one on film and the Kapo,[7] one on libel and customary proceedings in contexts of 'collaboration',[8] and one on criminal law and the Kapo.[9] Along this journey, this chapter juxtaposes the stories mounted by this play with other stories—vignettes and artefacts—recounted by (and through) diverse ways of remembering, recollecting, and sharing the iniquity of the death camps. Law—courtrooms, criminal trials, jailhouses— also serves as an alternate way to surface the agency of the persecuted when they persecute others. And, indeed, Israel turned to criminal trials to explicate Kapo violence. It did so in domestic courts in the 1950s and

[5] Galia Glasner-Heled and Dan Bar-On, 'Displaced: The Memoir of Eliezer Gruenbaum, Kapo at Birkenau—Translation and Commentary', *Shofar: An Interdisciplinary Journal of Jewish Studies* 27, no. 2 (Winter 2009): 1–23 at 2.

[6] Id. at 1.

[7] Mark A. Drumbl, 'The Kapo on Film: Tragic Perpetrators and Imperfect Victims', *Griffith Journal of Law & Human Dignity*, 27 no. 2 (2018): 229–271.

[8] Mark A. Drumbl, 'Histories of the Jewish "Collaborator": Exile, Not Guilt', in *The New Histories of International Criminal Law*, eds. Immi Tallgren and Thomas Skouteris (Oxford: OUP, 2019), available at https://papers.ssrn.com/sol3/papers.cfm?abstract_id=3009231.

[9] Mark A. Drumbl, 'Victims who Victimise', *London Review of International Law*, 4 no. 2 (2016): 217–246.

1960s. This chapter ends by glancing at these trials and by noting their struggles, including their crimped narrative ability. These trials experienced difficulties in coming to terms with the complexity and liminality of interstitial figures such as the Kapo.[10] Theater also struggles in this regard, to be sure, though less so it seems. Literary forms therefore can serve as lenses through which to look anew at international law; these forms can refresh; they may performatively help law reach some of its professed goals.

PLAY: OVERVIEW AND CHARACTERS

Bruno, the stage play's main character, came to Israel in 1946 together with his wife, Sarah. In real time, 470,000 Holocaust survivors came to Israel between the late 1940s and 1950s; these *arrivistes* comprised one-quarter of the nation's population.[11]

Bruno lives in Jerusalem. Rumors soon circulate that Bruno was an abusive Kapo. He is accused of being an SS collaborator and of having maltreated prisoners. In 1948 Bruno dies in the battle for kibbutz Ramat Rachel. Although not officially mentioned as such in the stage play, the timing is that this battle occurs in the 1948 Arab-Israeli War, part of what is also known in Israel as the War of Independence (1947–1949). Gruenbaum in real time died (was killed, took his own life) in this battle.

Set in Jerusalem, *Kapo in Jerusalem* takes the form of monologues delivered by a series of characters. There are 75 monologues in total. Each is numbered. Bruno's monologues occur at the end of May 1948 (in the battle in which he ultimately dies). The monologues of all the other characters—witnesses to Bruno's actions in the Auschwitz-Birkenau block—take place somewhat later, in 1950. The monologues are seen and heard by all other characters.

Bruno rationalizes his deployment of violence. According to Bruno, violence (*his* violence) was necessary to ensure that less overall violence occurred. Some of the other characters agree: they praise Bruno. Others, however, recoil at this suggestion. The overall synthesis, however, that is presented to the viewer is one of equivocation. Any and all certainties are ephemeral, evanescent, and constantly shifting. Sarah, Bruno's wife, delivers the most pained lines: weakened by doubt, coarsened by her own

---

[10] Ibid.

[11] Hanna Yablonka, 'The Development of Holocaust Consciousness in Israel: The Nuremberg, Kapos, Kastner, and Eichmann Trials', *Israel Studies* 8 no. 3 (Fall 2003): 1, 9.

perspective on what she did to survive, and soaked with concerns about their baby's future.

The choice to proceed through monologues imbues the play with great intimacy and intensity. This plot device allows the play to resemble a debate—bimodal, in one sense, but with multiple voices—thereby allowing the 'truth' to be approached from various personal perspectives.[12] Contrasting accounts of the same event fuel the play. Facts and conclusions are not to be found, they are to be felt. *Kapo in Jerusalem*'s characters speak freely without interruption, although when they speak they can be seen and heard by others and the characters react to each other. Hence, it becomes painfully clear how Bruno's attempts to defend himself tend to be delivered in vain to his skeptics or, at the least, how they fail to help his skeptics understand him better. Perhaps this explains Bruno's ultimate sacrifice. Perhaps Bruno himself found unconvincing his pleas that he was doing good by hurting others; or perhaps he simply recognized the futility of continuing to think and talk that way.

In the end, the reader is left in a profoundly ambiguous and interstitial place: according to a public discussion of the film, '[t]he resulting balance is so delicate that the viewer doesn't quite know what to think about Bruno'.[13] *Kapo in Jerusalem* excels at demonstrating 'just how difficult survival was in Auschwitz and the tragic and complex choices prisoners had to make as they negotiated the narrow divide between life and death in hell'.[14] The screenplay and film are described by Lerner as intending to 'put a question on Israeli society's past tendency to put Bruno on trial, not to defend his actions but to question his condemnation'.[15] Lerner adds that 'Israeli audiences are more open now to understanding the tragic

---

[12] This is the approach taken in Akira Kurosawa's film *Rashomon* (1950), in which four witnesses provide alternative versions of the same criminal incidents (the rape and murder of a couple). Heralded as a film of extraordinary quality, *Rashomon* underscores the subjectivity of truth and the vagaries of factual accuracy including in contexts of eye-witnessing; it has also been allegorically read as reflecting Japan's defeat in World War II.

[13] *Kapo in Jerusalem*, Holocaust Studies in Haifa, The Weiss-Livnat International MA Program in Holocaust Studies at the University of Haifa Blog (January 25, 2016) (accessed May 27, 2016, on file with the author).

[14] Id. It is not only Bruno who brings this forward, but also Sarah. At one point, she mutters: 'I stole bread from an aunt of mine with dysentery, knowing that in the morning she would die of hunger ... She didn't die. She stole bread from a woman who was weaker than her ... I met her again after the war ... She saw me ... and turned away' (29).

[15] Id.

nature of Bruno's role and more willing to recognize that it is difficult to understand, judge, and have empathy'.[16]

The following characters appear in *Kapo in Jerusalem*:

Bruno Kaminsky, a 40-year-old doctor who had served as a block leader in Auschwitz who ultimately dies in 1948 in armed conflict while trying to give medical treatment to a wounded soldier.

Sarah Reich, 36, a pianist and Auschwitz survivor who is Bruno's wife, and Bubu (their 18-month-old baby).

Karol Dubnov, 60, a physician who serves as chairperson of the Jerusalem Medical Association. Some of the characters in the play came to testify before Dubnov about Bruno's conduct at Auschwitz as part of an administrative sanction proceeding to expel Bruno from the medical association—the 'law' (the trial), so to speak.

Yulia Dubnov, 56, Karol's wife.

Meir Zimmerman, 45, a poet and Auschwitz survivor.

Anton Kinstler, 40, unemployed and Auschwitz survivor.

Dov Kovarshy, 45, manager of a pharmaceutical manufacturing plant and Auschwitz survivor.

Anshel Schwartz, 30, mentally ill and an Auschwitz survivor and among Bruno's more forceful defenders.

David Antman and Shmuel Wiessman, 56 and 35 respectively, both of whom also are Auschwitz survivors.

The shadow character, hidden throughout, is Eliezer Gruenbaum, who—in real time—was twice tried (outside Israel). One prosecution was brought before a communist tribunal; a second, in France, involved accusations by Jews. Both times Gruenbaun was found not guilty.[17] Gruenbaum was born in Poland. His father was a prominent Polish-Jewish politician who subsequently became Israel's first interior minister.[18] Gruenbaum was an ardent communist. He fought in Spain on the Republican side, and after the German invasion of France joined the French Resistance. He was arrested in 1942 as a communist and sent to Auschwitz-Birkenau, where

---

[16] Id.

[17] For further discussion of Eliezer Gruenbaum, see Tuvia Friling, *A Story of a Kapo in Auschwitz: History, Memory and Politics* (New Hampshire: University of New England Press, 2014).

[18] Glasner-Heled and Bar-On, *supra* note 5, at 1.

he became a Kapo.[19] He secured this 'appointment' through the intervention of the communists and served as 'the second in command to a sadistic Ukrainian commander of one of the barracks'.[20] At the same time he also 'joined the underground'.[21] Gruenbaum was removed in late 1943 to work in a coal mine, but returned to a concentration camp—Buchenwald—thereafter. Gruenbaum survived, though he was dogged by accusations—never fully dispelled by the acquittals and dismissals—that he mercilessly beat and killed Jewish prisoners. After his move to Israel, Gruenbaum was unable to hold down a job or sustain social relations—all because of his past. He was killed in battle. After his death, rumors spread that he had been shot in friendly fire out of revenge or that he had committed suicide. Gruenbaum's story is the basis for the play, and for Bruno.

Kapo in Jerusalem does not have scenes. The 75 monologues are numbered, but according to the playwright this is for 'simple identification during rehearsal'.

In guidance provided about acting out the stage play, it is indicated that the play only requires two actors on stage—one for Bruno and one for Sarah—with all the other characters being able to be videotaped and screened.

The stage play channels the position and placement of the characters. Each character is given a separate space, which is fixed in that they seldom leave it. Bruno's space is at the front of the stage—a military area prior to battle. The other characters are positioned behind him at a slight elevation. Sarah occupies the central space on that higher level, in the living room of her apartment, which she shares with a piano, couch, and baby's crib. Spaces, décor, and sound are urged to be minimalistic and sparse.

PLEATS AND PLOTS

Sarah opens the events. She plays Chopin while Bubu sleeps in a crib. Bruno, elsewhere, listens. Sarah frets about the baby. The 'welfare office', we cryptically learn, keeps an eye on them to ensure that the child is

---

[19] He arrived at Auschwitz in June 1942 and was sent a few days later to Birkenau. These two camps are adjacent to each other, though they form a whole that sprawls across the Polish countryside.

[20] Glasner-Heled and Bar-On, *supra* note 5, at 3.

[21] Id. (noting also that '[i]n the last days prior to the camp's [Buchenwald's] liberation [he] took part in self-defense actions directed against the SS').

healthy and not injured. This office causes Sarah great anxiety. We learn much later why the office is involved in Sarah and Bubu's life.

Bruno enters the play in battle while reminiscing about the Warsaw Ghetto, where 'we fought in streets' (4). Sarah tells the story of their meeting; Bruno chimes in with memories from Warsaw; Sarah opens up about their wedding after the war, in Dr. Dubnov's yard; Bruno, in turn, talks about his death march to Mauthausen.

Dr Dubnov and Yulia mention what an exceptional medical student Bruno was; they praise Sarah as a musical prodigy. Kovarsky underscores that Bruno was a surgeon in the Jewish underground: when Sarah was sent to Auschwitz, Bruno 'got hold of the two Jewish policemen who had captured her during the action. Rather than waste bullets, he broke their necks' (10). Bruno's capacity to deploy extreme violence, which narratively starts to unfurl here, is a thread that runs through the entire play.

Suspicions bubble to the surface. A postman delivering a wedding telegram identifies Bruno as a torturer; as a result, the rabbi refuses to conduct the wedding. Zimmerman, the poet and one of Bruno's foils, says that '[t]here was no bigger sadist than [Bruno] in the whole of Auschwitz' (12).

While battle rages in the distance, Bruno recalls that when he first 'got there, the prisoners suggested I be appointed to replace the blockfuhrer who had been killed by the SS. They knew that I was a doctor and that I'd been in the underground. They thought I'd be able to defend them against the Germans'. He then adds: 'I knew that blockfuhrer was part of the killing machine. But when I saw death run amok all around me, I knew I must pretend to be part of it, in order to save whoever I could' (13).

And so begins the tension between those who condemn Bruno and those—including himself—who struggle to rationalize his behavior: whether in pursuing the path of the lesser evil, or in pursuing the survivalist impulse. This tension, voiced through various characters on either side of the divide, propels the rest of the stage play in a taut to-and-fro.

Kovarsky exclaims: 'He hid the sick so they wouldn't be sent to the gas'. Kovarsky adds how Bruno falsified ages so that the SS would let people live; how he encouraged sabotage; 'helped everyone who wanted to escape' (15). Later, Bruno comments how he encouraged prisoners to escape, but the prisoners balked—according to Bruno, they refused because 'each was locked inside himself, hoping for a miracle', in particular that the war would end and that the Russians would arrive—so 'there was no point in escaping' (47). Bruno wryly remarks that '[t]he greatest cause of death in Auschwitz was hope'.

Zimmerman, Kinstler, and the Dubnovs underscore how Bruno beat prisoners, to which Bruno replies that the prisoners cluelessly had no idea where to stand or go. 'Had I not hit them, they would have been shot' by the SS (18). To wit:

> Yes, I beat prisoners during the morning roll call. [...] Everyone who was late had to be punished. I also beat those who didn't want to go to work. I knew that if they were caught in the block, they'd be sent straight to the gas. Those beatings saved their lives. (21)

With enemy fire whistling by, Bruno adds:

> I also beat prisoners who were too lazy to go to the latrines at night and pissed and shat in the food bowls. Going outside in the frost at night was more frightening than getting typhus or dysentery. (21)

Bruno demanded discipline when the food was handed out, or else chaos would have ensued. The power of hunger surfaces once again, as with the uncontrollability of the famished:

> One day, an SS officer sent me to Block 7 to get some musselmen[22] to repair fences that had collapsed under the snow. I told him that they were unable to move. He said: We'll soon see. And threw a few pieces of bread amongst them. The musselmen began crawling around for the bread. Those who were unable to move held out their arms in the hope that a piece would fall on them. One living corpse strangled another, to take some chewed crumbs from his mouth (23).[23]

Anshel speaks, praising Bruno for being an excellent thief who stole from the Germans: food, wood, even shoes and coats. While in a mental hospital, Anshel later affirms how Bruno will continue to look after him. This is because 'Bruno is a mensch'. Anshel recalls how when his father died 'there', he did so with a piece of bread in his pocket—when another inmate

---

[22] Or *Muselmänner*, 'literally, *Muslim*. A term used by prisoners of concentration camps for the prisoners suffering from extreme stages of starvation who were almost unable to move and spent much of their time cringing in a position similar to the one adopted by Muslims during prayer'. Glasner-Heled and Bar-On, *supra* note 5, at 5.

[23] Here Bruno echoes Gruenbaum, who also memorializes his own use of beatings in the name of safeguarding health, for example to thwart detainees from wearing the clothes of the dead at the risk of infecting the living. Id. at 16.

rushed to take it, 'Bruno saw it and forced him to give it to me' (44). Bruno also elicits praise for bringing soup that was thicker than the soup that others got, and for organizing shoe repairs—after all, '[i]f your shoes were broken and you began to limp, they immediately sent you to the gas' (27). Kovarsky adds how on one occasion Bruno was beaten because he had asked for wire-cutters and had unsuccessfully tried to escape.

Bruno implies that he killed the weakest of the *Muselmänner*—those who could not even drag themselves to the electric fences to kill themselves—and then hid their bodies so that he would be able to give 'their food to those who still had a chance' (33, 36). Bruno details how he 'shortened the suffering' of several *Muselmänner* in Auschwitz, and recalls the 'gratitude [he] saw in their eyes' (42). Finkelman says that Bruno told him to strangle two *Muselmänner* who were about to betray two Slovak Jews who planned to escape. Finkelman did so. 'Until today', Finkelman adds, 'I think it was the best thing I ever did. And until today I thank him, Bruno, for giving me the strength to do it' (37). As a physician, then, Bruno might be putting in place his training in triage, to save lives in accordance with the oath he would have taken. At times, this may mean giving up on those who are imminently lost. So for Bruno, this may seem natural and proper. For the poet Zimmerman, however, this appears repugnant and profoundly unnatural. The *Muselmänner* after all are still human beings. To view them with such contempt and worthlessness simply means that the prisoners have become socialized in the Nazi eliminationist ethos.

Yet, Sarah laments, Bruno (wrongly) thought 'that in Jerusalem, with all its survivors, they'd understand what he did there' (26). Bruno remarks how the complaints against him did not stop: one day he found 'Kapo' 'scribbled on [his] door at the clinic'. Gossip ensued. We later learn that Antman was the vandal.

What 'understanding' actually would entail remains very unclear. Antman, for example, reports that Bruno refused to let him aid his dying son so Antman had to helplessly listen to his son's dying groans all night long. Bruno responds that he did so because 'I knew that the SS would shoot him if he got near the boy'. He dismissively recognizes that Antman won't forgive him. Bruno quarrels with Dubnov, finding him 'unable to conceive of a world in which killing is an act of kindness. Where being compassionate means inflicting suffering' (40). Dubnov is actually quite empathetic in that he states that, after listening to Bruno speak, he 'understood that [he, Dubnov, doesn't] understand; that [he] can't understand'.

Dubnov adds: 'The witnesses against him were very persuasive, but so were his answers. I was unable to decide whether he acted to save himself of for the benefit of the prisoners' (41). Dubnov's inability to understand, once he is placed in the context of having to 'judge' (albeit in an administrative proceeding), reflects law's struggles to come to terms with the Kapo. These anxieties hobbled the Israeli Kapo trials in real time. Yet Dubnov still insists that the Jewish Agency should have 'established a special court to investigate all suspicions of collaboration with the Nazis', despite his inability to decide the much more mundane matter of whether or not to expel Bruno from the medical association. Dubnov recommends law when he personally found law unhelpful—but perhaps all will be well when the responsibility falls to others in a 'special' court.

Yulia, for her part, departs from her husband's sentiments. Her husband baffles her. Yulia affirms she was never 'fooled by [Bruno's] charm': she is ready to condemn him. Dubnov responds perfunctorily, telling her: 'Enough already! Please' (41). In a subsequent scene, with the tension between him and Yulia becoming palpable, Dubnov shares his regrets at having acquitted Bruno. He intuits that to acquit is as reductive as to convict. The binaries of law fail to satisfy—or even fit—at either end.

Bruno ultimately resigns from the clinic because, according to Dubnov, 'the suspicions against him were intolerable'. Sarah, too, faces recrimination at the conservatory.

So Bruno opens his own practice. One day Weissman comes with his wife who suffers from a throat infection. Weissman sees Bruno and rages. Weissman recalls how Bruno forced prisoners to shave beards and side-locks, forbade prayer, and beat them for praying; Bruno in fact sent a rabbi to his death. Calling Bruno a 'murderer', Weissman, his 'body [beginning] to boil', 'grabbed a pair of scissors and tried to stab him' until '[s]uddenly his wife appeared and began shouting' (52). As it turns out, Weissman succeeds in stabbing Bruno; when Bruno and Sarah are both back home, Sarah 'licked the blood from the wound, like we used to do there' (53). 'There' makes a frequent appearance to describe Planet Auschwitz, disembodied—a place and a space, suspended but also indelible. Bruno contemplates pressing charges against Weissman but ultimately refuses. He cycles back to his typical justificatory pattern: 'They didn't understand that I demanded they shave their beards and side-locks so the Germans wouldn't abuse them'. Bruno banned prayer putatively for protective purposes, namely, to safeguard the prisoners from being forced—if caught—to do 'exercises' until they 'collapsed' (54). Bruno notes that his critics Weissman, Zimmerman, and Kinstler survived the death march—along with 238 men from his block—this being a large number according to Bruno. He feels he deserves some credit for how he navigated all these horrors. Bruno, moreover (and ironically), brands Zimmerman as a 'petty SS informer' who, '[f]or a piece of bread, [...] informed on shirkers, on the sick, on thieves, on black marketers' (58).

Zimmerman beats Bruno one night as Bruno leaves his clinic, but stops short of death. That evening, home again, Bruno refuses to move elsewhere (which Sarah implores that they do): '[c]onvinced of his innocence ... leaving would be an admission of guilt' (59).

Weissman again becomes infuriated when he sees Bruno tearing pieces off a fresh loaf of bread on his way home from his clinic on another day. Weismann then burns Bruno's clinic, though he abstains from torching his house because of Sarah, coming as she does from a 'family of rabbis, all of whom died in Treblinka' (61). Again, Bruno refuses to go to the police, and balks at approaching any authorities. Bruno's refusal seems to be motivated by fear that any disclosure might trigger a criminal process in which Bruno would have to explain himself.

Sarah recalls becoming pregnant. She turns to the baby, smells a vomit stain on the sofa, takes a pill, begins to play piano loudly, the neighbor bangs on the walls, she curses him, and revisits her fear that the 'bitch' from the welfare office is coming tomorrow and will smell the stain and conclude that she is neglecting the child. It becomes apparent that Sarah is struggling. Bruno steps up. He puts on his military gear, and notes that they did not want the baby to stay in Israel, so that the child would not 'have to carry [Bruno's] hump on its back' (63). They try the USA. The American consular official is Jewish, and wonders how they survived the camps. 'It was clear that we had no chance', Bruno's voice trails off (63).

Sarah then relates, with anguish, how Bruno kills Mishka Weiss in an old Muslim cemetery after they leave the US consulate. Weiss had lain in wait there, with a pistol, but Bruno had his own pistol and shot first. Weiss is still alive, so Bruno finishes him off and steals his documents. Bruno was stunned that Weiss had survived Auschwitz. Before dying, Weiss yells that Bruno had sent him to the gas but he survived because the Nazis put him in a *Sonderkommando* unit in the crematorium at the last minute. Sarah adds:

> I was petrified. Not because of Mishka. Suddenly, I saw in Bruno a cruelty that I had never seen before. Which I didn't believe he had in him. (64)

Sarah recounts how Bruno had told her that Mishka was violent in the camp, had killed prisoners for bread and shoes, that Mishka had attacked him with planks, leaving a scar on his face. Left untouched is the irony that Bruno killed the weakest for shoes and bread in order for others to survive, and Sarah survived by theft as well. Sarah concludes, speaking of Bruno:

I listened to him. I understood him. But I also feared him. (64)

We learn later that Antman paid Mishka to kill Bruno, but then Antman expresses relief that Mishka failed (without commenting on how Mishka's failure led to such a tragic outcome):

I'm a victim and I'm a witness. But I'm not a judge. I'm certainly not a hangman. The state has to pass a law that will bring people like him to trial sentence them to death and execute them. (65)

Once again, the play evokes the pull of law and wish for law, while also making it clear that persons like Bruno roam beyond law's capacities. The hunger for law fails to satiate. 'We' crave law, yet law leaves 'us' unfilled and unfulfilled.

Bruno comes into focus, deriding Mishka as a 'disgusting killer' (66). He recognizes that something changed that night in Sarah; she looks away, her face telling him that he was 'too quick to shoot him … other people's lives aren't worthless' as they were in Auschwitz (66).

Attempts to secure visas fail dismally all around. Bruno notes that Sarah could have gotten one only for her and for the child. But she refused. War breaks out. Bruno enlists. Sarah knows why—he does so to die. She breaks down. She vomits 'everything she swallowed'—returning to the theme of the sofa and the baby. Bruno persists. Sarah tells the enlistment office that he had been a Kapo, an SS collaborator, and that he was a murderer in Jerusalem. She tries to shoot herself. Bruno stops her, hugs her, takes his own pistol out of her hands. The enlistment office refuses to register him. But then Dubnov helps, later on. Dubnov intervenes.

On the battlefield, Bruno knows. He knows that '[s]he wanted to kill herself because she understood that I would never be clean in her eyes' (70). She knows because 'she had been there' (70). But then he adds, with incredulity:

Doesn't she understand that they are blaming me to cover up their own cowardice, their own helplessness and wretchedness, their self-disgust and their shame? I, who tried to save them, I am responsible for their suffering and degradation? I am responsible for their deaths? (72)

Dubnow cries at home. Yulia tries to stay with Sarah after her suicide attempt so as to safeguard the baby. Yulia had had a daughter, Dina, who died in the war.

Kovarsky learns of the news. He goes to Sarah. She slams the door in his face. 'Since then, I send her packages on the holidays. Food. Clothes. Toys ...' (74).

Sarah brings the stage play to a close. She recounts the circumstances of Bruno's death in an Arab ambush. He was running tall to help a wounded soldier. 'He ran to him, his body upright, despite the fire and the shelling. He knew why he was running upright' (75). And then:

It was difficult for me to care for the child after the birth. Sometimes, I cried so much that I couldn't hear him crying. Then they came from the welfare office and took him to some kibbutz. I went after them and snatched him back. I knew that I couldn't go on living without him. Since then, I hardly cry ...

Now, a Turn to Law

Kapo in Jerusalem does not involve Bruno, or others, denying that violence occurred. Nor does it involve Bruno denying that he was a perpetrator of violence. At no point does he say, colloquially speaking, that he 'didn't do it'. *Kapo in Jerusalem* is about the mental element (i.e. why?) and about the defense of necessity (i.e. because it was just, or understandable in the circumstances). It is also about other things that Bruno did—good things—that some of the survivors either do not know or overlook (whether deliberately or inadvertently). Still, not even one time does Bruno engage in any circumspection that perhaps his skeptics have something meaningful to say or that their perceptions have some genuineness. Bruno relentlessly rationalizes that he killed but 'it's okay' because those he killed were suffering or that in the deaths of the lifeless the living could eke out a better chance at survival. He thereby presents his violence as the lesser evil. He defines himself as making the most out of an impossible situation. He is the tragic figure. That said, left unresolved is whether

Bruno was violent to protect others or, rather, to protect himself from other prisoners or from the Nazis.[24] His motivation may have been his own survival. On the other hand, Bruno later ends his own life. He takes his own life because he sees no future for himself and, moreover, to remove the burden—the weight of his shame, the 'hump'—from the shoulders of his family. Bruno dies in the fight for Israel's independence, but his death is utterly inconsequential for the lives of others.

After the establishment of the state of Israel in 1948, Jewish 'collaborators'—*kapos*, ghetto police, and officials who negotiated with Nazis—were seen as particularly confronting characters: so much so that the Knesset enacted criminal legislation (the *Nazi and Nazi Collaborators Punishment Act*) in 1950 to 'cleanse' them from Israel.[25] This legislation embodied many political goals, and channeled the hunger of victims—victims of the acts of collaborators, victims of the violent acts of other victims—for justice by opening an official space for them to tell their stories. Insofar as there were no Nazis in Israel at the time, the purpose of the law was to target Jewish Holocaust survivors suspected of collaboration. The only German Nazi tried under this law was Adolf Eichmann. John Demjanjuk, a Ukrainian-born concentration camp guard SS volunteer who had been captured by the Germans as a prisoner-of-war, also was tried under this law in the late 1980s.[26] He was prosecuted following his deportation to Israel from the USA (where he had emigrated and was an auto worker). The dénouement of the Demjanjuk proceedings proved an 'embarrassment' to

---

[24] Brown, *'No one will ever know'*, supra note 2, at 99 (noting that '*Kapos* were subject to punishment by Nazi guards for any problems arising from their charges and Jewish *Kapos* were arguably under more pressure to keep their positions through violence').

[25] Orna Ben-Naftali and Yogev Tuval, 'Punishing International Crimes Committed by the Persecuted: The *Kapo* Trials in Israel (1950s-1960s)', *Journal of International Criminal Justice* 4 (2006): 129 at 141, 144, 147 (noting that 'the Law had as its primary target Jewish collaborators, who were themselves persecuted persons' and that it was 'primarily designed to realize, indeed, to constitute a community of "pure victims"' and to 'cleans[e] the Jewish community in Israel of Jewish traitors').

[26] Demjanjuk ultimately was acquitted in Israel on charges of having been a guard at Treblinka. In 2011 he was tried and convicted in Germany as an accessory to mass murder as a guard at Sobibór. He appealed but died during the appeal process. Hence, his conviction was never validated. The legal theories deployed to try Demjanjuk in Germany have nonetheless inspired other subsequent prosecutions of former concentration camp guards and officials. For his part, Demjanjuk argued that he was like a Jewish *Kapo*—that he should be seen as a victim injured by the Nazis.

Israel's legal system; the *Nazi and Nazi Collaborators (Punishment) Law* has since remained unused.[27]

The Israeli Justice Minister had presented the *Nazi and Nazi Collaborators (Punishment) Law* to the first Knesset as follows:

> We may safely assume that Nazi criminals ... will not venture to Israel, but the law also applies to those who implemented the Nazis' will, and unfortunately some of them may be in our midst ... Hopefully the proposed law will contribute to cleansing the air among the survivors who have immigrated to Eretz Israel.[28]

The Law included an array of offenses. The major offenses, which entailed a mandatory death sentence, were crimes against the Jewish people, crimes against humanity, and war crimes. The legislation proscribed five other offenses: crimes against persecuted persons, offenses in places of confinement, delivering persecuted persons to enemy administration, blackmailing persecuted persons, and membership in an enemy organization. These latter offenses did not trigger the death penalty. Only one of the Jewish defendants was ever found guilty of a major offense. No Jewish defendant was charged with crimes against the Jewish people.[29] The crime of 'offenses in places of confinement' (article 4(a) of the legislation) was specifically designed to deal with Kapo actions in ghettos and concentration camps that fell short of major crimes.[30] The Law did not formally distinguish between the Nazis and their collaborators, even when collaborators were persecuted persons. The Law's quest for condemnation, finitude, and clarity effectively constructed the persecuted Jew as a Nazi, thereby dispelling any 'gray zone'.

Authorities conducted approximately 40 prosecutions. The legislator's unwillingness to legally distinguish Nazis from persecuted collaborators proved too crude. The criminal law failed in its attempt to conceptualize Kapo violence. Law lacked the vocabulary or finesse; the courtroom was a poor conduit. Many of the records of the Kapo proceedings have been

---

[27] Michael Bazyler and Julia Scheppach, 'The Strange and Curious History of the Law Used to Prosecute Adolf Eichmann', *Loyola of Los Angeles International and Comparative Law Review*, 34 (2012): 417 at 418, 461 ('Though it remains officially on the books, the law is a dead letter').

[28] Statement of Pinhas Rosen, cited in Yablonka, *supra* note 11 at 11.

[29] Ben-Naftali and Tuval *supra* note 25 at 153.

[30] Id. 136.

sealed at the behest of the families of the accused (for 70 years as of the time of the judgment). Records of other proceedings were destroyed in a flood. Documentation nonetheless exists regarding 23 of the Kapo indictments: nine of these ended up in acquittals following a trial, 14 in convictions.[31] The average sentence was 17 months; one convict was sentenced to 10 years' imprisonment. Acquittals proved as unfulfilling as convictions.

Debates about the lifelessness of the still living—Bruno's turn to the *Muselmänner*—resonated in the celebrated 1884 case of *R. v Dudley and Stephens*, involving survival cannibalism on the yacht *Mignonette* after it sank upon the high seas.[32] The English courts, keen to end what had been an occupational custom of the sea, held that necessity could not be a defense for a charge of murder, even among the castaways and shipwrecked when one among them fell into a coma (as was the case with the cabin-boy Richard Parker on the *Mignonette*, an analogue perhaps to Bruno's *Muselmänner*). Parker was killed and cannibalized only after the turnips had run out, one turtle had been eaten (including the bones), and the only thing left to drink was urine. In this regard, then, the common law may well be with Zimmerman. Indeed Dudley and Stephens were initially sentenced to death, but the sentence was commuted to six months in prison. This chestnut case sounds a bit like the Kapo trials, gnarly and oscillating, thereby indicative of the awkwardness of the criminal law in such situations.

Positionality is a key window into Bruno's soul. He vacillates between treating the prisoners as a 'they' (in the 'there' of Auschwitz)—from his perspective—and as a 'we'. These very same shifting identities infuse Gruenbaum's memories. While after the fact it may be comforting for Gruenbaum to self-identify with prisoners, during actual camp life such identification assured a faster death. Being part of the oppressors, however, would be too much: membership in the alternate 'we' of the camp overlords festered in the criminal proceedings because it meant being a Nazi. This was too much weight for the law to bear. Glasner-Heled and Bar-On scope out a third category, namely, that of 'observer from within the belly of the beast', which they read as one that Gruenbaum also self-adopts from time to time. They unspool how this shift in pronouns—this role-playing—fills some of the memoir's passages, for example

---

[31] Itamar Levin, *Kapo on Allenby Street* (Yad Ben Tzvi & Moreshet Publications, 2015).

[32] [1884] 14 Q.B.D. 273 (Eng.); see generally A.W. Brian Simpson, *Cannibalism and the Common Law* (1984).

Gruenbaum's description of food distribution: 'Every person knew that they, too, were destined to die of hunger. Consequently, you had to eat, at all costs! We were not distributing milk—we were distributing life'.[33]

CONCLUSION

Holocaust trials—which require actual accuseds and witnesses—are rapidly shrinking in number and nature as time passes. The powerful dramaturgy of such moments—for example, the Eichmann trial—is no longer possible. This leaves the reenactment, including on stage, as one way to intersect law with the living, including in cases such as the Kapo trials in which actual proceedings proved problematic. As time continues to pass, these alternate ways of staging—alternate to courtrooms in real time—will emerge more decidedly as one way to recall, remember, and relive. Such reenactments are becoming all the more important. In 2018, on Holocaust Remembrance Day, a survey was published that indicated that 41 percent of Americans, and 66 percent of millennials, 'cannot say what Auschwitz was'.[34] This is not because of denialism. It is because of forgetting, of 'receding from memory'.[35] International law's future, in terms of the violence of the past, may hinge on storytellers who range well beyond the legal scene. What results, then, is storytelling about and around law, not through and within law: *staging* law rather than *enforcing* law.

BIBLIOGRAPHY

Astor, Maggie. Holocaust Is Fading from Memory, Survey Finds. *New York Times*, April 12, 2018.

Bazyler, Michael, and Julia Scheppach. 2012. The Strange and Curious History of the Law Used to Prosecute Adolf Eichmann. *Loyola of Los Angeles International and Comparative Law Review* 34: 417.

Ben-Naftali, Orna, and Yogev Tuval. 2006. Punishing International Crimes Committed by the Persecuted: The *Kapo* Trials in Israel (1950s–1960s). *Journal of International Criminal Justice* 4: 129.

Brown, Adam. 2015. *Judging "Privileged" Jews: Holocaust Ethics, Representation and the "Grey Zone"*. Oxford: Berghahn.

---

[33] Glasner-Heled and Bar-On, *supra* note 5, at 21.

[34] Maggie Astor, 'Holocaust is Fading From Memory, Survey Finds', *New York Times* (April 12, 2018).

[35] Id.

Drama Israel. Kapo in Jerusalem. http://dramaisrael.org/wp-content/uploads/2014/12/Kapo-in-Jerusalem-September-2014.pdf.

Drumbl, Mark A. 2016. Victims Who Victimise. *London Review of International Law* 4 (2): 217–246.

———. 2018. The Kapo on Film: Tragic Perpetrators and Imperfect Victims. *Griffith Journal of Law & Human Dignity* 27 (2): 229–271.

———. 2019. Histories of the Jewish "Collaborator": Exile, Not Guilt. In *The New Histories of International Criminal Law*, ed. Immi Tallgren and Thomas Skouteris. Oxford: OUP. Available at https://papers.ssrn.com/sol3/papers.cfm?abstract_id=3009231.

Friling, Tuvia. 2014. *A Story of a Kapo in Auschwitz: History, Memory and Politics.* New Hampshire: University of New England Press.

Glasner-Heled, Galia, and Dan Bar-On. 2009. Displaced: The Memoir of Eliezer Gruenbaum, Kapo at Birkenau – Translation and Commentary. *Shofar: An Interdisciplinary Journal of Jewish Studies* 27 (2, Winter): 1–23.

Kurosawa, Akira. 1950. *Rashomon.* Minoru Jingo.

Levi, Primo. 1988. *The Drowned and the Saved.* 1st ed. Trans. Raymond Rosenthal. London: Michael Joseph.

Levin, Itamar. 2015. *Kapo on Allenby Street.* Yad Ben Tzvi & Moreshet Publications.

Marrus, Michael. 1987. *The Holocaust in History.* New York: Penguin.

Simpson, A.W. Brian. 1984. *Cannibalism and the Common Law: A Victorian Yachting Tragedy.* Chicago: University of Chicago Press.

Yablonka, Hanna. 2003. The Development of Holocaust Consciousness in Israel: The Nuremberg, Kapos, Kastner, and Eichmann Trials. *Israel Studies* 8 (3, Fall): 1.

CHAPTER 4

A Story that Can(not) be Told: Sexual Violence against Men in ICTR and ICTY Jurisprudence

Thomas Charman

One of the overarching themes of this volume, as discussed by Stolk and Vos in Chap. 1, is that the practice of international law, and indeed law in general, is not a simple and uncomplicated pathway to an objective and truthful outcome. Rather, it is a bricolage of stories, both told and untold, that open up and make possible particular understandings and courses of action, whilst simultaneously closing off others. As such, considering the silences and silencing practices of international law becomes ever more important, to see what is 'left out' of legal stories. In this chapter, I explore this theme through the prism of sexual violence against men in armed conflict, an issue that has only recently started to be addressed in law, policy, and research on abuses during times of war. Using written trial and sentencing judgements produced by the International Criminal Tribunals for Rwanda (ICTR) and the former Yugoslavia (ICTY), I deconstruct the ways in which these tribunals have structured the terrain of sexual violence discourse in such ways as to obscure, highlight, or marginalise the

T. Charman (✉)
University of Edinburgh, Edinburgh, UK

© The Author(s), under exclusive license to Springer Nature Switzerland AG 2020
S. Stolk, R. Vos (eds.), *International Law's Collected Stories*, Palgrave Studies in International Relations, https://doi.org/10.1007/978-3-030-58835-9_4

problem, how they have (or have not) told the story of sexual violence against men within this discursive terrain, and what the legal consequences of these stories may be.

I argue that the existing jurisprudence on sexual violence against men from the ICTR/Y is characterised by ambiguity. At times, the stories told through and by the written legal judgements produced by the Trial Chambers are contradictory or inconsistent; at others, the stories converge with the more familiar stories of sexual violence against women. Sometimes the problem is entirely absent from stories of sexual violence, and sometimes instances of sexual violence against men are relayed in stories of other crimes, such as torture or cruel and inhuman treatment. This ambiguity is reflected in the jurisprudence on sexual violence more broadly, as the two principal approaches to defining rape and sexual violence, those in *Akayesu* and *Furundžija*, differ in their ability to adequately cover instances of sexual violence against men. Furthermore, I argue that the choice of story has legal consequences; telling a story of sexual violence against men that frames the violence as, for example, non-sexual torture risks suppressing alternative narratives and structuring jurisprudence in such a way as to inhibit the possibility of re-visualising and prosecuting such violence as specifically sexual in the future.

The chapter proceeds as follows. The first section provides a brief overview of the problem of sexual violence against men in armed conflict and considers the problem in the context of its relationship with international law through an engagement with the existing literature. The second section draws on this existing literature and conceptualises international legal tribunals as discursive bodies that play a role in actively constituting the subjects and objects with which they concern themselves. This section also briefly addresses the theoretical and methodological foundations of the chapter. The third section tells the story of the evolution of ICTR/Y case law pertaining to sexual violence against men in armed conflict and addresses some of the tensions and ambiguities of the jurisprudence that has emerged from both *Akayesu* and *Furundžija*. The fourth section examines in more detail the case law of the ICTR/Y and the contradictory ways in which the story of sexual violence against men has been told through the various written judgements produced by the tribunals. The fifth section considers the possible legal consequences of these contradictory stories of sexual violence against men. In particular, it notes the role of jurisprudence in informing understandings of crime-categories, and how telling the story of sexual violence against men as, for example, a form of torture may complicate efforts to prosecute such forms of violence specifically as sexual violence in the future. The chapter concludes with some reflections on the problems posed by the ambiguities of stories of sexual violence against men promulgated by international criminal tribunals for attempts to more fully recognise and address the problem.

SEXUAL VIOLENCE AGAINST MEN IN ARMED CONFLICT: A BRIEF OVERVIEW

Sexual violence in armed conflict has remained a subject of significant interest on the agendas of international human rights agencies and organisations since the issue was first brought to prominence as a result of highly effective feminist campaigns for change during the late twentieth century.[1] However, this advocacy and policy activity has largely focused on sexual violence against women and girls. A growing body of scholarship has noted, first, the existence and widespread use of sexual violence against men in past and ongoing conflicts and, second, the frequent marginalisation of the problem in mainstream discourses of sexual violence in armed conflict.[2] Whilst recent years have seen a surge in advocacy, policy, and research activities dedicated to the subject, sexual violence against men has largely remained a periphery concern.

Despite the widespread occurrence of such violence, international legal statutes and tribunals have yet to fully address the problem. Whilst ostensibly covered by existing provisions within the Rome Statute and the jurisprudence of past ad-hoc international tribunals that also cover sexual violence against women,[3] Dustin Lewis has argued that, in practice, international law does not adequately cover, prosecute, or punish acts of

---

[1] Lara Stemple, 'Male Rape and Human Rights', *Hastings Law Journal* 60 (2009): 626.

[2] See, for example, Sandesh Sivakumaran, 'Sexual Violence Against Men in Armed Conflict', *European Journal of International Law* 18, no. 2 (2007); Marysia Zalewski et al., eds., *Sexual Violence against Men in Global Politics* (Abingdon: Routledge, 2018); Dubravka Zarkov, 'The Body of the Other Man: Sexual Violence and the Construction of Masculinity, Sexuality and Ethnicity in Croatian Media', in *Victims, Perpetrators or Actors: Gender, Armed Conflict and Political Violence*, ed. Caroline O. N. Moser and Fiona Clark (London: Zed Books, 2001), 69–82.

[3] Hilmi Zawati, 'Impunity or Immunity: Wartime Male Rape and Sexual Torture as a Crime against Humanity', *Journal on Rehabilitation of Torture Victims and Prevention of Torture* 17, no. 1 (2007).

sexual violence against men.[4] This is highlighted by the recent rejection of evidence pertaining to sexual violence against men and boys in the *Ongwen* case at the International Criminal Court (ICC).[5] In those cases where sexual violence against men and boys has been included in the charges, Solange Mouthaan has noted that the tendency to prosecute acts of sexual violence against men and boys under the rubric of torture rather than sexual violence—such as in the *Tadić* decision[6]—serves to problematically synonymise sexual violence with torture and elides any gendered element of the crime.[7]

INTERNATIONAL LAW AND THE ROLE OF LANGUAGE

Central to these critiques of the relationship between sexual violence against men and international criminal law is an understanding that legal language has power. Sandesh Sivakumaran, on the subject of the frequent framing of sexual violence against men as torture, argues that:

> There is a need to recognise the general—rape as torture, as well as the particular—rape as rape. An accurate classification of abuse is important not just to give victims a voice, not only to break down stereotypes and not merely to accurately record the picture. Language in general and legal language in particular 'reinforces certain world views and understandings of events … Through its definitions and the way it talks about events, law has the power to silence alternative meanings—to suppress other stories'. It is essential that these stories not be suppressed.[8]

Sivakumaran's argument is predicated upon an understanding of language as constitutive, rather than neutrally reflective, of the world around us. His arguments resonate with those who reject the idea that law, and

---

[4] Dustin Lewis, 'Unrecognized Victims: Sexual Violence Against Men in Conflict Settings Under International Law', *Wisconsin International Law Journal* 27, no. 1 (2009): 1.

[5] Rosemary Grey, Jonathan O'Donohue, and Leonard Krasny, 'Evidence of Sexual Violence against Men and Boys Rejected in Ongwen', *Human Rights in International Justice* (blog), 10 April 2018, https://hrij.amnesty.nl/evidence-sexual-violence-men-boys-rejected-ongwen/.

[6] Kelly Askin, 'Sexual Violence in Decisions and Indictments of the Yugoslav and Rwandan Tribunals: Current Status', *The American Journal of International Law* 93, no. 1 (1999): 102.

[7] Solange Mouthaan, 'International Law and Sexual Violence against Men' (Warwick: University of Warwick School of Law, 2012), 3.

[8] Sivakumaran, 'Sexual Violence against Men in Armed Conflict', 256–57.

the language deployed within it, is objective and neutral, and instead adopt an approach where legal language is conceptualised as ontologically significant.[9] For example, Finley argues that:

> Language, and the thoughts that it expresses, is socially constructed and socially constituting. Rather than being neutral or naturally ordained, it reflects the world views and chosen meanings of those who have had power to affect definitions and create terms. The selected terms and meanings then shape our understandings of what things are, of the way the world is.[10]

A growing body of scholarship has examined the ways in which legal language shapes understandings of crimes. For example, Brenda Danet notes the ways in which the use of certain forms of language over others, specifically the use of the term 'baby' instead of 'fetus', in the case of a US obstetrician performing an abortion resulted in a verdict of manslaughter.[11] The underlying theme of these studies is that language is *constitutive* of the world around us, rather than merely reflective. As such, legal writing takes on a discursive character. This is concisely summarised by Coates, Bavelas, and Gibson:

> There is an obvious but underdeveloped affinity between discourse analysis and the practice of law. Language and texts are central to the practice of law, which can be said to primarily consist of discourse. Written judgements, in particular, *express* the state of law at any given time. Furthermore, they *affect* not only the litigants but also the future shape of the law and society at large. The language used in legal judgements is not merely a reflection of individual thought; it is important in and of itself.[12]

---

[9] Janet Beavin Bavelas and Linda Coates, 'Is It Sex or Assault? Erotic Versus Violent Language in Sexual Assault Trial Judgements', *Journal of Social Distress and the Homeless* 10, no. 1 (2001); John M. Conley and William M. O'Barr, *Just Words: Law, Language, and Power*, Second Edition (University of Chicago Press, 2005); Brenda Danet, 'Language in the Legal Process', *Law & Society Review* 14 (1979); Peter Goodrich, *Legal Discourse: Studies in Linguistics, Rhetoric and Legal Analysis* (Springer, 1990).

[10] Lucinda M. Finley, 'Breaking Women's Silence in Law: The Dilemma of the Gendered Nature of Legal Reasoning', *Notre Dame Law Review* 64 (1989): 887.

[11] Brenda Danet, '"Baby" or "Fetus"?: Language and the Construction of Reality in a Manslaughter Trial', *Semiotica* 32, no. 3–4 (1980).

[12] Linda Coates, Janet Beavin Bavelas, and James Gibson, 'Anomalous Language in Sexual Assault Trial Judgements', *Discourse & Society* 5, no. 2 (1994): 189, emphasis in original.

Building on this argument, I propose that a discourse-centred analysis of legal language and the constitutive power of the law holds significant potential for understanding how stories of sexual violence against men have been told in both the ICTR and ICTY. A poststructuralist-informed methodology is particularly appropriate in this context; as Lene Hansen argues, 'to poststructuralism, language is ontologically significant: it is only through the construction in language that 'things'—objects, subject, states, living beings, and material structures—are given meaning and endowed with a particular identity'.[13] The analytical approach of the chapter is akin to what Howarth refers to as a 'strategy of problematisation',[14] whereby the goal is not to 'fact check' international legal discourses, but rather to 'draw out and comment on the 'regimes of truth' operant in this discursive terrain'.[15] I draw heavily on Laura Shepherd's Discourse-Theoretical Analysis (DTA), in which she suggests locating and identifying a variety of articulatory practices in the text. She divides these practices into two categories. The first she describes as 'the forms of thought or linguistic structures that provide a sense of order in the texts, thus constructing the meaning of the concepts with which I am concerned'.[16] For this category, she gives the examples of certain signifiers described 'as' or 'like', statements that can be problematised, and emphasise concepts provided either by repetition or their placement within the text.[17] The second category she describes as 'the articulation of subjects and objects'.[18] The documents subjected to this analysis consist of 18 judgements from the ICTY and 12 from the ICTR in which sexual violence, or violence that could be understood as sexual (such as violence towards the genitals), was mentioned. These documents were subject to several read-throughs, and were coded according to the principles of Shepherd's DTA. For example, instances of text where the meaning of 'sexual violence' was modified through predication or emphasised through prominent placement were

[13] Lene Hansen, *Security as Practice: Discourse Analysis and the Bosnian War* (London: Routledge, 2006), 18.

[14] David Howarth, *Discourse* (London: Open University Press, 2000), 135.

[15] Laura J. Shepherd, *Gender, Violence, and Security: Discourse as Practice* (London: Zed Books, 2008), 31.

[16] Shepherd, 30.

[17] Shepherd, 30.

[18] Shepherd, 30.

coded and tagged. The codes were then grouped thematically to aid the teasing out of overall themes and to assist in structuring the analysis section of the chapter.

COMPETING DEFINITIONS: THE EVOLUTION OF SEXUAL VIOLENCE CASE LAW IN THE ICTR AND ICTY

The starting point of the DTA of the written judgements produced by the ICTR and ICTY was not an analysis of the stories of sexual violence against men themselves, although this later formed the bulk of the analysis conducted; rather, it began with a consideration of the conditions that enabled these stories to be told in the first place, what Michel Foucault referred to as 'conditions of possibility'.[19] Poststructuralists place a particularly heavy emphasis on understanding those conditions that structure and enable the intelligibility (or unintelligibility) of discourse; Laclau notes that the analysis of discourse is 'a type of analysis primarily addressed not to facts but to their conditions of possibility. The basic hypothesis of a discursive approach is that the very possibility of perception, thought and action depends on the structuration of certain meaningful field which pre-exists any factual immediacy'.[20] As such, the analysis began with a consideration of how the case law concerning the definition of sexual violence has evolved since the mid-1990s. Interpretations of acts, the *actus reus* and *mens rea* of particular crimes, serve a categorising function; they codify both what can be and, implicitly, what cannot be considered as falling into the category of a particular crime. As such, the evolution of case law, its structuring of the discursive field in which the written judgements operate, and the implications it has for whether sexual violence against men can actually be categorised as 'sexual violence' or 'rape'—thus determining whether the story can or cannot be told—take on a new significance.

Whilst the precise definition of rape and sexual violence in armed conflict has been subject to much negotiation and contestation within and across written judgements since the inception of the ICTR and ICTY, two broad approaches have emerged: the *Akayesu* decision, and the *Furundžija*

---

[19] Michel Foucault, *The Order of Things: An Archaeology of the Human Sciences*, Routledge Classics (London: Routledge, 2002), xxiv.

[20] Ernesto Laclau, 'Discourse', in *A Companion to Contemporary Political Philosophy*, ed. Robert E. Goodin, Philip Pettit, and Thomas Pogge, Second Edition (Oxford: Blackwell Publishing Ltd, 2007), 541, emphasis in original.

and *Kunarac* decisions. *Akayesu* represents the first instance of an international criminal conviction for rape and sexual violence and was the first case to constitute rape as a form of genocide. The decisions of the *Akayesu* Trial Chamber on the elements and definition of rape and sexual violence are worth reproducing in full:

> 597. The Chamber considers that rape is a form of aggression and that the central elements of the crime of rape cannot be captured in a mechanical description of objects and body parts … Like torture, rape is used for such purposes as intimidation, degradation, humiliation, discrimination, punishment, control or destruction of a person. Like torture, rape is a violation of personal dignity, and rape in fact constitutes torture when inflicted by or at the instigation of or with the consent or acquiescence of a public official or other person acting in an official capacity.
>
> 598. The Chamber defines rape as a physical invasion of a sexual nature, committed on a person under circumstances which are coercive. Sexual violence, which includes rape, is considered to be any act of a sexual nature which is committed on a person under circumstances which are coercive.[21]

> The Tribunal considers sexual violence, which includes rape, as any act of a sexual nature which is committed on a person under circumstances which are coercive. Sexual violence is not limited to physical invasion of the human body and may include acts which do not involve penetration or even physical contact.[22]

This stands in marked contrast to *Furundžija* and *Kunarac*. The *Furundžija* Trial Chamber, the first to focus specifically on sexual violence, and *Kunarac*, which drew heavily on *Furundžija*, explicitly rejected the *Akayesu* findings on rape and sexual violence[23] and instead defined them thusly:

> 185. Thus the Trial Chamber finds that the following may be accepted as the objective elements of rape:
>   The sexual penetration, however slight:

---

[21] The Prosecutor v. Jean-Paul Akayesu (Judgement), ICTR-96-4-T (International Criminal Tribunal for Rwanda 1998), para. 597–598.

[22] *Akayesu*, para. 688.

[23] Prosecutor v. Anto Furundžija (Judgement), IT-95-17/1-T (International Criminal Tribunal for the Former Yugoslavia 1998), para. 185–186.

Of the vagina or anus of the victim by the penis of the perpetrator or any other object used by the perpetrator; or

Of the mouth of the victim by the penis of the perpetrator

By coercion or force or threat of force against the victim or a third person
186. As pointed out above, international criminal rules punish not only rape but also any serious sexual assault falling short of actual penetration. It would seem that the prohibition embraces all serious abuses of a sexual nature inflicted upon the physical and moral integrity of a person by means of coercion, threat of force or intimidation in a way that is degrading and humiliating for the victim's dignity.[24]

The *Akayesu* and *Furundžija/Kunarac* definitions of sexual violence and rape diverge from each other significantly. Whereas *Akayesu* was widely lauded for its broad definition and abstention from defining rape and sexual violence purely in mechanical or biological terms,[25] *Furundžija* and *Kunarac* instead opted to define rape purely on the basis of 'sexual penetration' and the presence of coercion. By defining rape as a form of 'physical invasion of a sexual nature', and also bringing in the non-consent or coercion of the victim, *Akayesu* arguably opened up the scope of acts which could be conceived of and charged as rape. This includes male victims, given that to be charged as rape, an act only requires a physical invasion of a sexual nature and that the victim does not consent. Unlike some more mechanical definitions of rape, where body parts are specified, *Akayesu* does not imply or assume the sex of the perpetrator or victim. Furthermore, its broad definition of sexual violence, in that physical contact is not required as an element of sexual violence, conceivably allows for an even broader scope of acts to be classified as sexual violence, such as enforced nudity or masturbation, where the intent is sexualised and there is no consent, but the act would otherwise not fit under other more mechanical definitions. Furthermore, similarly to the findings on rape, the absence of any predication of the act of rape or sexual violence on any gender-specific pronouns or physical characteristics ostensibly provides scope for the application of this particular definition of rape and sexual

---

[24] *Furundžija*, para. 176–177.

[25] Suzanne Chenault, 'And Since Akayesu? The Development of ICTR Jurisprudence on Gender Crimes: A Comparison of Akayesu and Muhimana', *New England Journal of International and Comparative Law* 14, no. 2 (2008); Caleb J. Fountain, 'Sexual Violence, the Ad Hoc Tribunals and the International Criminal Court: Reconciling Akayesu and Kunarac', *ILSA Journal of International and Comparative Law* 19 (2012): 253.

violence to male victims as well as female victims. In terms of its impact on the discursive terrain of sexual violence discourse, *Akayesu* arguably enables more and varied stories of sexual violence to be told within the Trial Chambers.

In contrast, the *Furundžija* and *Kunarac* decisions are problematic when considering sexual violence against men. The repetition of the term 'penis' when describing the objects used by the perpetrator to inflict the violence on the victim, despite the absence of sex-specific pronouns, serves to implicitly constitute the body of the perpetrator as male. This is problematic given that both men and women commit acts of sexual violence during armed conflict,[26] and later decisions of the ICTY, such as *Karadžić*, would find that acts of sexual violence against both women and men were perpetrated by women as well as men. The implicit rendering of perpetrators as male serves to reinforce a female victim/male perpetrator dynamic within the decisions that elides acts of violence that do not adhere to this binary. Furthermore, the *Furundžija* and *Kunarac* decisions base their findings on the elements of rape and sexual violence on a reading of domestic statutes concerning rape.[27] In many cases, these definitions of rape are explicitly predicated upon a male perpetrator and female victim. In some instances, decisions that have drawn upon the *Furundžija* and *Kunarac* definition have made this binary more explicit. For example, the *Kvočka* Trial Chamber, when setting out the elements of rape, asserts:

> The Trial Chamber agrees with the factors set out by the Trial Chamber in *Kunarac*, defining rape as a violation of sexual autonomy. In order for sexual activity to be classified as rape:
> The sexual activity must be accompanied by force or by threat of force to the victim or a third party;
> The sexual activity must be accompanied by force or a variety of other specified circumstances which made the victim particularly vulnerable or negated *her* ability to make an informed refusal; or
> The sexual activity must occur without the consent of the victim.[28]

---

[26] Laura Sjoberg, *Women as Wartime Rapists: Beyond Sensation and Stereotyping* (New York: New York University Press, 2016).

[27] *Furundžija*, para. 177–178; Prosecutor v. Dragoljub Kunarac et al. (Judgement), IT-96-23-T (International Criminal Tribunal for the Former Yugoslavia 2001), para. 443–456.

[28] Prosecutor v. Miroslav Kvočka et al. (Judgement), IT-98-30/1-T (International Criminal Tribunal for the Former Yugoslavia 2001), para. 177, emphasis added.

The predication of victim on gender-specific pronouns (in this case, 'her') constitutes the victim as female and discursively eliminates the space for stories of sexual violence where the victim is male. Similarly, the *Gacumbitsi* decision notes that:

> The Chamber is of the opinion that any penetration of the victim's vagina by the rapist with his genitals or with any object constitutes rape, although the definition of rape under Article 3(g) of the Statute is not limited to such acts alone.[29]

Here, the perpetrator is explicitly constituted as male (through use of the term 'his genitals') and the victim as female, with the association between 'victim' and 'vagina'. Although *Gacumbitsi* acknowledges that the definition of rape is not just limited to these acts, the choice to foreground and explicitly state this particular definition of rape serves to emphasise this particular configuration of the act, namely a specifically male perpetrator and a specifically female victim. As such, the *Furundžija* and *Kunarac* definitions, and the decisions that draw on the case law established by them, serve to complicate the discursive terrain by providing a competing and more specific definition of rape and sexual violence that arguably limits the space in which such violence towards men can be articulated, either through implicitly constituting the body of the perpetrator as male and the victim as female, or, in some cases, explicitly constructing the victim as female and the perpetrator as male.

AMBIGUOUS STORIES: SEXUAL OR NON-SEXUAL VIOLENCE?

The different approaches to conceptualising sexual violence embodied by *Akayesu* and *Furundžija/Kunarac* throw into sharp relief the ambiguity that surrounds the position of, and potential for articulating, sexual violence against men within the context of international law. However, this ambiguity in the discursive terrain does not necessarily preclude stories of sexual violence against men being told, nor does it preclude the conceptualisation of this form of violence as a specifically sexual crime. In contrast, however, there are numerous instances in which violence against men that could be interpreted as sexual in nature is not articulated as a sexualised

---

[29] The Prosecutor v. Sylvestre Gacumbtsi (Judgement), ICTR-2001-64-T (International Criminal Tribunal for Rwanda 2004), para. 321.

form of violence, but rather, for example, as a form of torture or ill-treatment. This section documents instances of both of these stories of sexual violence within the written judgements.

Stories of Sexualised Violence

Stories where violence against men, such as rape and sexual abuse, is explicitly constituted, described, and charged as sexualised violence are somewhat scarce in the written judgements. Nevertheless, they are present within the case law of the ICTR/Y. To take but a few examples, the recent *Karadžić* decision describes multiple instances of Bosnian Muslim men and women being raped and sexually assaulted by Bosnian Serb soldiers and guards or forced to engage in sexually degrading acts, either with each other or with other guards:

> When one of his female relatives was taken away, a male detainee tried to follow her but could not; he was later taken by two men to the cellar and shown where she had been raped ... he was also raped two and a half weeks after being detained; he was brought to the basement at least 30 times and raped on almost every occasion. He was tied to a desk, he was verbally abused, pliers were used to mistreat him, and he was raped by police truncheons and similar objects.[30]

> Other acts of sexual violence included male and female detainees who were ordered to undress, dance, and perform sexual acts in front of Bosnian Serb soldiers. In other incidents detainees were forced to remove their underwear and bite or suck each other's penises while soldiers stood by and laughed. In another incident detainees were forced to lick the buttocks of a Bosnian Serb woman, who threatened to slit their throats if they did not comply.[31]

The Chamber subsequently found that 'Bosnian Muslim women, men, girls, and boys were subject to rape and other acts of sexual violence'[32] as a form of cruel and inhuman treatment, itself a form of persecution. This decision is surprising in the way it constitutes sexual violence against men and boys in relation to sexual violence against women and girls when considered in the context of the past marginalisation or exclusion of men and

---

[30] Prosecutor v. Radovan Karadžić (Judgement), IT-95-5/18-T (International Criminal Tribunal for the Former Yugoslavia 2016), para. 991.

[31] *Karadžić*, para. 2506.

[32] *Karadžić*, para. 2506.

boys from sexual violence discourse; no particular distinction is made between sexual violence against women and men beyond the use of pronouns to indicate the sex of the victim and the different forms that the violence took, in contrast to some earlier decisions. As such, the text equates sexual violence against men with sexual violence against women, articulating the possibility of both women and men as victims and survivors of rape and sexual violence.

Another example is to be found within the *Bagosora* decision. In describing acts of violence that occurred at a roadblock in Kigali, the decision notes that:

> These [civilian roadblocks] were sites of open and notorious slaughter and sexual assault. Several witnesses, including Dallaire and Beardsley, observed dead men and women around roadblocks throughout Kigali, including children. The bodies of the dead were frequently piled near the roadblocks and at times were collected by local officials. Female victims were left lying on their back with their legs spread and stained with semen. Dallaire saw objects crushed or implanted in vaginas, breasts cut off, stomachs opened and the mutilated genitals of men.[33]

The location of descriptions of violence towards the genitals of men next to descriptions of sexual violence towards women, and the predication of all of these descriptions on the term 'sexual assault' towards the beginning of the excerpt, serves to constitute violence towards men's genitals as a sexualised form of violence. Whilst the Trial Chamber was not convinced beyond reasonable doubt that the defendants were directly or indirectly responsible for these acts, the telling of the events in this particular way remains discursively significant.

One final example is to be found in the *Mucić/Čelebići* decision, where the Trial Chamber finds that the act of forcing two men to perform fellatio on each other constitutes a crime against humanity:

> The Trial Chamber finds that the act of forcing Vaso Đorđić and Veseljko Đorđić to perform fellatio on one another constituted, at least, a fundamental attack on their human dignity. Accordingly, the Trial Chamber find that this act constitutes the offence of inhuman treatment under Article 2 of the Statute, and cruel treatment under Article 3 of the Statute. The Trial

---

[33] The Prosecutor v. Théoneste Bagosora et al. (Judgement), ICTR-98-41-T (International Criminal Tribunal for Rwanda 2008), para. 1908.

Chamber notes that the aforementioned act could constitute rape for which liability could have been found if pleaded in the appropriate manner.[34]

It is interesting to note the tone of near-reproach in the text; whilst the acts were ultimately charged as inhuman treatment and cruel treatment, the Trial Chamber notes that the act of enforced fellatio would satisfy the requirements for rape. As such, whilst the violence itself is classified under different charges, the interjection by the Trial Chamber serves to reinforce the act of enforced fellatio as an act of specifically sexual violence, namely rape.

Stories of the Non-Sexual

Whilst the discursive terrain established by the decisions of the ICTY and ICTR does provide space for stories of violence against men to be told as instances of specifically sexual violence, as shown above, this does not ensure that these kinds of stories will always be told. In many instances, the kinds of stories that are told about sexual violence against men in armed conflict are told in such a way as to elide or diminish the potentially sexualised dimension of the violence the victims experience. For example, the *Mucić* decision describes an instance of trauma inflicted on the genitals:

> In a detailed account of this event, Mirko Đordić described how Esad Landžo removed Vukašin Mrkajić's trousers and placed a slow-burning fuse against his bare skin around his waist and genitals. He ordered the victim to put the trousers back on, whereupon he set light to the fuse … the Trial Chamber finds that the intentional act of placing a burning fuse cord against Vukašin Mrkajić's bare body caused the victim such serious suffering and injury that it constitutes the offence of wilfully causing great suffering or serious injury to body or health under Article 2, and cruel treatment under Article 3 of the Statute.[35]

Violence towards the genitals is one of the more common sexual crimes experienced by men during armed conflict.[36] However, this particular pas-

---

[34] Prosecutor v. Zdravko Mucić et al. (Judgement), IT-96-21-T (International Criminal Tribunal for the Former Yugoslavia 1998), para. 1066.

[35] *Mucić* et al., para. 1038–1040.

[36] Eric Stener Carlson, 'The Hidden Prevalence of Male Sexual Assault during War: Observations on Blunt Trauma to the Male Genitals', *The British Journal of Criminology* 46, no. 1 (2006).

sage instead constitutes trauma towards the genitals as aimed at causing great suffering and serious injury—the violence is not articulated as having a sexual dimension. Whilst violence towards the genitals certainly causes significant suffering and injury, the decision, in constituting it in this manner, closes off avenues for also considering this violence as potentially sexual. For example, Zarkov notes that violence towards the penis may have ethnic and gendered dimensions, whereby it is both a signifier of the virility of the male and the virility of the nation.[37] Considering the extreme ethnic dimension that characterised the wars in the former Yugoslavia, the elision of the sexual or gendered dynamics underpinning certain forms of violence may rob us of valuable insights into the meanings that lie behind their infliction. Further examples where the violence towards men is predicated as a non-sexual infliction of pain or humiliation include the *Simić*, *Hategekimana*, and *Brđanin* decisions:

> Counts 7, 8 and 9 charge that one night in June 1992, in the hallway of the gymnasium of the Bosanski Samac primary school, Milan Simić kicked and beat Safet Hadžialijagić, and placed the barrel of his gun in Safet Hadžialijagić's mouth. While Milan Simić kicked and beat him, other men repeatedly pulled down Safet Hadžialijagić's pants and threatened to cut off his penis.[38]

> Witness QCL testified that people's identity cards were checked at the roadblocks in order to verify their ethnicity and that, as a Tutsi, he was beaten, searched, disrobed and insulted by soldiers from the Ngoma Camp throughout the genocide on a daily basis.[39]

> On 26 June 1992, Omarska camp guards tried to force Mehmedalija Sarajlić, an elderly Bosnian Muslim, to rape a female detainee. He begged them "Don't make me do it. She could be my daughter. I am a man in advanced age." The guards laughed and said "Well, try to use the finger." A scream and the sound of beatings could be heard, and then everything was silent. The guards had killed the man. The Trial Chamber, by majority, finds that the threat of rape constituted a sexual assault vis-à-vis the female detainee.[40]

[37] Zarkov, 'The Body of the Other Man'.

[38] Prosecutor v. Milan Simić (Sentencing Judgement), IT-95-9/2-S (International Criminal Tribunal for the Former Yugoslavia 2002), para. 4.

[39] The Prosecutor v. Ildephonse Hategekimana (Judgement), ICTR-00-55B-T (International Criminal Tribunal for Rwanda 2010), para. 186.

[40] Prosecutor v. Radoslav Brđanin (Judgement), IT-99-36-T (International Criminal Tribunal for the Former Yugoslavia 2004), para. 516.

The final excerpt is particularly notable from a discursive viewpoint. It is interesting to note here that the threat of rape made against the victim is articulated as sexual assault, but not the threat to force someone to rape, which could be considered as rape or sexual assault under existing case law, particularly *Akayesu*. Similarly to violence against the genitals, some forms of violence that could be constituted as being sexual in nature—in this case, trying to force someone to rape another—are not articulated as sexual assault.

Legal Necessity and the Silencing of Alternative Stories

Why do the articulations of these stories matter? It is tempting to argue that as long as the perpetrator is convicted of a crime in some manner for acts of sexual violence, the need for justice has been satisfied. Indeed, feminist scholar Catharine MacKinnon has previously argued that rape in armed conflict should be reconceptualised and prosecuted as torture in order to take advantage of the comparatively more stringent international and national legal sanctions attached to the crime of torture.[41] Given that sexual violence against men has historically been marginalised and still occupies a precarious place in international criminal law, illustrated most recently by the rejection of the *Ongwen* Trial Chamber of evidence relating to sexual violence against men and boys,[42] the telling of these stories as torture, or as instances of cruel and inhuman treatment, may represent a more reliable route to a conviction.

However, telling the story of sexual violence, against both men and women, as torture or cruel and inhuman treatment has legal consequences. Securing a conviction for torture or cruel and inhuman treatment requires the story of the experiences of the victim to be told in such a way as to conform to the parameters of these crimes set out in the statutes on which international criminal tribunals are founded and the body of case law established by previous Trial Chambers. However, each crime-category is necessarily distinct from the others; the crimes of rape and sexual assault have different parameters and requirements for *mens rea* and *actus reus*

---

[41] Catherine MacKinnon, *Are Women Human? And Other International Dialogues* (Cambridge, MA: Harvard University Press, 2006), 17.

[42] Grey, O'Donohue, and Krasny, 'Evidence of Sexual Violence against Men and Boys Rejected in Ongwen'.

than torture or cruel and inhuman treatment. For example, the *Furundžija* decision requires that, for an instance of violence to fit into the crime-category of sexual assault, it must constitute a 'serious [abuse] of a sexual nature',[43] although what constitutes a 'sexual nature' goes curiously undefined. By contrast, torture is constituted as 'the infliction of ... severe pain or suffering, whether physical or mental'.[44] There is no requirement for the violence to be articulated as being sexual in nature in order to conform to the parameters of torture. Conversely, violence must be articulated as specifically sexual in nature in order to qualify as sexual assault. The charging of acts that could be construed as sexual violence as a form of torture therefore opens up the possibility that the story of this violence excludes or omits any sexual dimension to the acts, changing their meaning. Whilst, as discussed in the previous section, there are instances in which Trial Chambers have charged acts as torture or cruel or inhuman treatment whilst also articulating them as sexual in nature (such as in *Mucić*), this is by no means guaranteed. There are numerous instances in which acts of violence against men are told without reference to the possibly sexualised or gendered nature of that violence, effectively erasing this potential facet of the violence from the story.

Jurisprudence informs legal understandings of crime-categories and the forms of violence that fit into those categories. In this context, the tendency to prosecute acts of what may be construed as sexual violence against men—whether consciously, as a means of securing a conviction, or unconsciously as a consequence of a lack of awareness or understanding that certain forms of violence men suffer in armed conflict may be sexual or gendered in nature—as a form of torture or cruel or inhuman treatment is problematic. As the trend continues and more jurisprudence emerges that tells the story of, to take but one example, blunt force trauma directed towards the genitals as a form of torture or cruel treatment rather than sexual assault, this further informs understandings of crime-categories and forms of violence that may be articulated within the parameters of these categories, thus fortifying this approach and potentially making it harder to convict perpetrators for sexual assault. This is further complicated by jurisprudence on the parameters of the crime-categories themselves; as discussed previously, the definitions of rape and sexual assault given in *Furundžija* and *Kunarac* shape the discursive terrain in such a

---

[43] *Furundžija*, para. 186.
[44] *Furundžija*, para. 162.

way that complicates the inclusion of male victims within these crime-categories in the first place.

Herein lies the tension at the heart of prosecuting sexual violence against men in armed conflict in international criminal tribunals. The prosecution of these crimes under alternative crime-categories is an innovative means of providing justice to victims who have historically been marginalised or even deliberately excluded from consideration. For example, the *Tadić* decision, one of the first judgements rendered by the ICTY in 1997, found Dusko Tadić guilty of cruel and inhuman treatment for forcing prisoners to mutilate the genitals of, and ultimately castrate, another prisoner. This represented the first conviction for an instance of sexual violence against men, albeit as cruel and inhuman treatment, and one that preceded the convictions for rape in the *Akayesu* decision of the ICTR the following year. However, the subsequent accumulation of jurisprudence that articulates sexual violence against men, such as inflicting trauma to the genitals, as a form of torture or cruel and inhuman treatment begins to erase the possibility of telling the story of these crimes as sexual assault or rape in court.

Furthermore, the necessity in the legal process to articulate stories in such a way as to enable them to fit the parameters of a particular crime-category comes into conflict with the need to create a space for the victims of violence to tell their stories and to fully conceptualise the nature of the violence being prosecuted. Ultimately, legal necessity arguably trumps the need to provide a space for victims, given that narratives provided by victims must be shaped by the prosecution in order to fulfil the criteria required for a conviction. This, as Janine Clark argues, creates silences in the stories:

> Legal trials are quintessentially about facts—who did what to whom, when, where, how? Hence, while they create a space for witnesses to recount their stories, this storytelling is strictly controlled and driven by the needs of the court. This means that legal judgements necessarily contain silences.[45]

Taking this into account, it becomes clear that legal language does not just hold the *potential* to, as Sivakumaran puts it, 'silence alternative

---

[45] Janine N. Clark, 'Masculinity and Male Survivors of Wartime Sexual Violence: A Bosnian Case Study', *Conflict, Security & Development* 17, no. 4 (2017): 291.

narratives [and] suppress other stories';[46] it is actually essential to the process of law. As such, Sivakumaran's imperative to tell the story of both torture-as-rape and rape-as-rape[47] becomes more complex; the re-visualisation of the stories from ICTR/Y Trial Chambers accrues greater importance as a consequence of the need to uncover what is obscured or marginalised by the way in which these stories are told. But it also invites a broader critique of international criminal law and, given the legal necessity of suppressing alternative narratives, its role as a teller of stories and history.

CONCLUSIONS

The findings presented in this chapter represent some initial analytical forays into how stories of violence that have historically been marginalised and overlooked have been told in and by the Trial Chambers of the ICTR/Y, and what the legal consequences of the choice of stories may be. It is difficult to identify one overarching story of sexual violence against men that is told consistently across the decisions; rather, the corpus of case law produced by the ICTR/Y resembles more a bricolage of competing and negotiated definitions and stories that serve to provide multiple perspectives on the problem of sexual violence against men. This particular form of violence is rendered variously as visible or invisible, as sexual or non-sexual, or as possible or impossible, depending on the particular instance of case law one looks at. Ultimately, the dominant theme that comes across from a reading of the case law as a whole is ambiguity. Whilst there is undoubtedly a space for male victims of sexual violence within the framework of the *Akayesu* approach to sexual violence, this is less clear when considering the preponderance of the *Furundžija* and *Kunarac* framework in the case law. This ambiguity is further complicated by variations in the stories told in and by individual Trial Chambers, with some constituting the violence as specifically sexual violence, and others subsuming it into the broader categories of non-sexual torture or ill-treatment.

Where does this leave sexual violence against men in armed conflict and international criminal law more broadly? Certainly, the ambiguity in terms of the stories told of sexual violence against men is problematic, in the sense that it may stymie access to justice for victims. Furthermore, these stories have legal consequences, and may serve to both reinforce the

---

[46] Sivakumaran, 'Sexual Violence against Men in Armed Conflict', 257.

[47] Sivakumaran, 257.

elision of the potentially sexualised element of various forms of violence suffered by men in armed conflict and potentially inhibit future attempts to charge these forms of violence as sexual violence. The legal necessity of suppressing alternative narratives and stories throws into turmoil the role of international criminal tribunals as both storytellers and tellers of history; if all stories told in and by Trial Chambers contain silences or suppress alternative ways of telling them as a legal necessity, then their established accounts of violence within the context of armed conflict represent only one possible discursive interpretation of these acts. For sexual violence against men, a subject that has historically been under-reported, the framing of such violence as only torture may serve to further exacerbate the perception that this is a rare occurrence in armed conflict.

This is, however, not to dismiss entirely the stories and jurisprudence that emerge from such trials. Whilst the ambiguity is problematic, it also demonstrates that stories of violence *can* be visualised as stories of specifically sexual violence. Indeed, the convictions of rape and sexual assault secured for acts of violence against both men and women, particularly within the *Karadžić* decision, represent a significant step away from the previous obscurity of sexual violence in armed conflict prior to the 1990s, and arguably an increasing trend of securing such convictions. Furthermore, these prosecutions demonstrate that, within the constraints of existing jurisprudence on the subject, there is scope for a re-visualisation of these stories that could take into account both their use as a form of torture and their status as acts of sexualised violence, to, as Sivakumaran argues, 'recognise the general—rape as torture, as well as the specific—rape as rape'.[48] However, it remains necessary to interrogate and re-visualise these stories in order to ensure that alternative accounts, narratives, and stories do not become the victims of legal necessity.

BIBLIOGRAPHY

Askin, Kelly. 1999. Sexual Violence in Decisions and Indictments of the Yugoslav and Rwandan Tribunals: Current Status. *The American Journal of International Law* 93 (1): 97–123.

Bavelas, Janet Beavin, and Linda Coates. 2001. Is It Sex or Assault? Erotic Versus Violent Language in Sexual Assault Trial Judgements. *Journal of Social Distress and Homeless* 10 (1): 29–40.

---

[48] Sivakumaran, 256–57.

Carlson, Eric Stener. 2006. The Hidden Prevalence of Male Sexual Assault during War: Observations on Blunt Trauma to the Male Genitals. *The British Journal of Criminology* 46 (1): 16–25.

Chenault, Suzanne. 2008. And Since Akayesu? The Development of ICTR Jurisprudence on Gender Crimes: A Comparison of Akayesu and Muhimana. *New England Journal of International and Comparative Law* 14 (2): 221–237.

Clark, Janine N. 2017. Masculinity and Male Survivors of Wartime Sexual Violence: A Bosnian Case Study. *Conflict, Security and Development* 17 (4): 287–311.

Coates, Linda, Janet Beavin Bavelas, and James Gibson. 1994. Anomalous Language in Sexual Assault Trial Judgements. *Discourse & Society* 5 (2): 189–206.

Conley, John M., and William M. O'Barr. 2005. *Just Words: Law, Language, and Power*. 2nd ed: University of Chicago Press.

Danet, Brenda. 1979. Language in the Legal Process. *Law and Society Review* 14: 445–564.

———. 1980. "Baby" or "Fetus"?: Language and the Construction of Reality in a Manslaughter Trial. *Semiotica* 32 (3–4): 187–220.

Finley, Lucinda M. 1989. Breaking Women's Silence in Law: The Dilemma of the Gendered Nature of Legal Reasoning. *Notre Dame Law Review* 64: 886–910.

Foucault, Michel. 2002. *The Order of Things: An Archaeology of the Human Sciences*. Routledge Classics. London: Routledge.

Fountain, Caleb J. 2012. Sexual Violence, the Ad Hoc Tribunals and the International Criminal Court: Reconciling Akayesu and Kunarac. *ILSA Journal of International and Comparative Law* 19: 251–262.

Goodrich, Peter. 1990. *Legal Discourse: Studies in Linguistics, Rhetoric and Legal Analysis*. Springer.

Grey, Rosemary, Jonathan O'Donohue, and Leonard Krasny. 2018. Evidence of Sexual Violence against Men and Boys Rejected in Ongwen. *Human Rights in International Justice* (blog), 10 April. https://hrij.amnesty.nl/evidence-sexual-violence-men-boys-rejected-ongwen/.

Hansen, Lene. 2006. *Security as Practice: Discourse Analysis and the Bosnian War*. London: Routledge.

Howarth, David. 2000. *Discourse*. London: Open University Press.

Laclau, Ernesto. 2007. Discourse. In *A Companion to Contemporary Political Philosophy*, ed. Robert E. Goodin, Philip Pettit, and Thomas Pogge, 2nd ed., 541–547. Oxford: Blackwell Publishing Ltd.

Lewis, Dustin A. 2009. Unrecognized Victims: Sexual Violence Against Men in Conflict Settings Under International Law. *Wisconsin International Law Journal* 27 (1): 1–49.

MacKinnon, Catharine. 2006. *Are Women Human? And Other International Dialogues*. Cambridge, MA: Harvard University Press.

Mouthaan, Solange. 2012. *International Law and Sexual Violence against Men*. Warwick: University of Warwick School of Law.

Shepherd, Laura J. 2008. *Gender, Violence, and Security: Discourse as Practice*. London: Zed Books.

Sivakumaran, Sandesh. 2007. Sexual Violence against Men in Armed Conflict. *European Journal of International Law* 18 (2): 253–276.

Sjoberg, Laura. 2016. *Women as Wartime Rapists: Beyond Sensation and Stereotyping*. New York: New York University Press.

Stemple, Lara. 2009. Male Rape and Human Rights. *Hastings Law Journal* 60: 605–646.

Zalewski, Marysia, Paula Drumond, Elisabeth Prügl, and Maria Stern, eds. 2018. *Sexual Violence against Men in Global Politics*. Abingdon: Routledge.

Zarkov, Dubravka. 2001. The Body of the Other Man: Sexual Violence and the Construction of Masculinity, Sexuality and Ethnicity in Croatian Media. In *Victims, Perpetrators or Actors: Gender, Armed Conflict and Political Violence*, ed. Caroline O.N. Moser and Fiona Clark, 69–82. London: Zed Books.

Zawati, Hilmi. 2007. Impunity or Immunity: Wartime Male Rape and Sexual Torture as a Crime against Humanity. *Journal on Rehabilitation of Torture Victims and Prevention of Torture* 17 (1): 27–47.

CHAPTER 5

The Desire to be an International Law City: A Self-Portrait of The Hague and Amsterdam

Lisa Roodenburg and Sofia Stolk

Cities desire to become associated with international law. The Hague presents itself as the 'City of Peace and Justice', while Amsterdam profiles itself as a 'Human Rights City'. This turn to international law could be explained by several motives: the persuasive authority of international norms,[1] the need for guidance in dealing with urban challenges,[2] economic and networking benefits,[3] or by way of legitimizing local policies that deviate from

---

[1] Janne Nijman, "Renaissance of the City as Global Actor. The role of foreign policy and international law practices in the construction of cities as global actors," in *The Transformation of Foreign Policy: Drawing and Managing Boundaries from Antiquity to the Present*, ed. Gunther Hellmann, Andreas Fahrmeir and Miloš Vec (Oxford Scholarship Online, 2016).

[2] Nijman, ibid.

[3] Barbara Oomen, Martha F. Davis and Michele Grigolo, "Introduction: The rise and challenges of human rights cities," in *Global Urban Justice: the rise of human rights cities*, eds. Barbara Oomen, Martha F. Davis and Michele Grigolo (Cambridge: Cambridge University Press, 2016).

L. Roodenburg (✉) • S. Stolk
T.M.C. Asser Institute / University of Amsterdam, The Hague, The Netherlands
e-mail: l.roodenburg@asser.nl; s.stolk@asser.nl

© The Author(s), under exclusive license to Springer Nature Switzerland AG 2020
S. Stolk, R. Vos (eds.), *International Law's Collected Stories*, Palgrave Studies in International Relations,
https://doi.org/10.1007/978-3-030-58835-9_5

the national stance.[4] Concurrently, the association with international law is also a matter of image building, which is the focus of this chapter. Cities locate themselves in international law, and in doing so, they define their normative affiliations. These normative affiliations allow cities to position themselves vis-à-vis their inhabitants and the world.

This chapter discusses the self-portrayal of The Hague and Amsterdam as international law cities and investigates how international law is deployed as a key feature to construct a self-image and reach a certain audience. The relation between cities and international law is often discussed in terms of practical or economic advantages, by focusing on what cities gain from the engagement with international law while they are not considered international legal personalities.[5] We approach this relation differently: we explore what is desired by such normative positioning through the lens of the self-portrait. In doing so, we want to shift our focus to a more symbolic, social and aesthetically motivated rationale behind a city's image building efforts.

The self-image of cities is most frequently discussed in the academic literature under the heading of 'city marketing' or 'city branding'.[6] In short, city branding entails associating and selecting different attributes or images with a city, packaged in a marketing message. City branding is used as an instrument to generate economic investments and a competitive position, as well as to put forward an identity inhabitants can relate to.[7] The performance of city brands has been critically evaluated, for example because these brands often put forward a message that might not represent all inhabitants, but favour local elites.[8] Furthermore, economic objectives are often placed centre stage, while the inhabitants come in second

---

[4] Nijman, "Renaissance of the City."; Helmut Aust, "Shining Cities on the Hill? The Global City, Climate Change, and International Law," *The European Journal of International Law* 26, no.1 (2015): 255–278.

[5] Yishai Blank, "The City and the World," *Columbia Journal of Transnational Law* 47, no.686 (2006): 875–939.

[6] Mihalis Kavaratzis, "From city marketing to city branding: Towards a theoretical framework for developing city brands," *Place Branding* 1, no.1 (2004): 58–73.; Graham Hankinson and Pilippa Cowking, *Branding in action: cases and strategies for profitable brand management* (McGraw-Hill, 1993), 10.; Mihalis Kavaratzis and Gregory Ashworth, "City Branding: an effective assertion of identity or transitory marketing trick?," *Tijdschrift voor Economische en Sociale Geografie* 96, no.5 (2005): 10.

[7] Kavaratzis, "From city marketing to city branding"; Kavaratzis & Ashworth, "City Branding."

[8] Ari-Veikko Anttiroiko, "City Branding as a Response to Global Intercity Competition," *Growth and Change* 46, no.2 (2015): 233–252.

place.[9] Stigel and Frimann underscore that when the link between the outward 'economic attractiveness' message and the inward 'community building' message is not established, the result will be experienced as an empty promise and a disconnect with urban reality.[10] However, despite the expansion of the critical city branding literature, most studies are still limited to assessing the 'success' of city brands, rather than exploring the variety of motives and desires that are involved in a city's image building practices. Hence our turn to the self-portrait lens.

In art history, self-portraits have interestingly enough long been regarded as primarily economically motivated products too, mainly serving purposes of self-promotion and means to commission new assignments. For this reason, the genre has, at times, been treated as inferior to other artistic genres. However, following Crozier and Greenhalgh, we wish to emphasize the plurality of motives behind self-portraiture, including, for example, the wish to deepen self-knowledge, to make an artistic statement, to vent narcissism, to continue a historical tradition or the practical convenience of having your subject always at hand.[11]

A self-portrait is a performance that entails both 'taking a certain stance towards the self'[12] and constituting the self in relation to others.[13] In Cumming's words: 'whatever they show of the outer person, self-portraits speak of the inner self too in the character and choice of depiction'.[14] This conflict of interests inherent in a self-portrait resembles the tension between serving internal and external audiences that characterizes a city's image building practices. It is simultaneously an exercise in introspection and a form of communication to the outside world. These two roles are not necessarily reconcilable. However, we do not see this as a problem; rather, we aim to explore the potential tensions and uncertainties around audience perception as a key characteristic of image building, without proposing solutions for a 'better' or 'more truthful' portrait. Self-portraiture

---

[9] Maria Cristina Paganoni, "City Branding and Social Inclusion in the Glocal City," *Mobilities* 7, no.1 (2012): 13–31.

[10] Jørgen Stigel and Søren Frimann, "City Branding – All Smoke, No Fire?," *Nordicom Review* 2 (2006): 245–268.

[11] Ray Crozier and Paul Greenhalgh, "Self-Portraits as Presentations of Self," *Leonardo* 21, no.1 (1988): 30.

[12] Crozier & Greenhalgh, "Self-Portraits as Presentations of Self'," 29.

[13] Amelia Jones, "The "Eternal Return": Self-Portrait Photography as a Technology of Embodiment," *Signs* 27, no.4 (2002): 950.

[14] Laura Cumming, *A Face to the World: on Self-Portraits* (William Collins, 2014), 5.

is not only about crafting a realistic or appealing image of the self. These images are specialized in other kinds of truths: 'no matter how fanciful, flattering or deceitful the image, it will always reveal something deep and incontrovertible (...) namely this special class of truth, this pressure from within that determines what appears as art without, that leaves its trace in every self-portrait'.[15] The self-portrait lens therefore allows us to see the image building efforts of a city not only as a cold strategy but as a *desire* to be portrayed and perceived in a certain way.[16]

The remainder of this chapter discusses the making of a self-portrait in two cities that actively engage with international law: The Hague and Amsterdam. At first glance, The Hague tends to rely on international law mainly for its outward image, while Amsterdam draws specifically on human rights law for both international and local audiences. However, from our analysis of The Hague as 'City of Peace and Justice' and Amsterdam as 'Human Rights City', a more complex and perhaps confused picture arises. We draw on municipal policy documents and four in-depth interviews with municipality staff members—of The Hague's Bureau Citybranding, The Hague's International Affairs Department, Amsterdam's International Office and Amsterdam's Program Diversity—who work on and with the city's self-image on a daily basis.

THE HAGUE: CITY OF PEACE AND JUSTICE

The Hague explicitly connects itself to international law by adopting the slogan 'City of Peace and Justice'. The city has a long history of promoting its international relevance by attracting international organizations and events such as the Peace Conferences in 1899 and 1907.[17] In the same period, the Permanent Court of Arbitration (PCA) took its seat in The Hague and acquired a permanent premise in the newly built Peace Palace, where the PCA and the International Court of Justice still reside. The active acquisition of international organizations really took off in the

---

[15] Cumming, "A Face to the World," 3.

[16] Jones, "The "Eternal Return'"; Cumming, 'A Face to the World."

[17] Bengt Arne Hulleman and Robert Govers, "The Hague, International City of Peace and Justice" in *City Branding*, ed. Keith Dinnie (London: Palgrave Macmillan, 2011): 152; Herman van der Wusten, "'Legal Capital Of The World': Political Centre-Formation In The Hague," *Tijdschrift voor Economische en Sociale Geografie* 97, no. 3 (2006): 256; Christine Schwöbel-Patel, *Marketing Global Justice: The Political Economy of International Criminal Law* (Cambridge University Press, 2021, forthcoming).

1990s and The Hague's role as legal capital of the world got a definitive boost when it successfully campaigned for hosting the ad-hoc International Tribunal for the Former Yugoslavia in 1993 and the permanent International Criminal Court in 2002.[18]

Historically, the Dutch Ministry of Foreign Affairs played the leading role in the international ambitions of the city,[19] but in 2006 the municipality itself established Bureau Citybranding, a specialized department that focuses on the marketing and branding of The Hague. Since then, international justice has become more and more emblematic in the city's image building strategy. Bureau Citybranding, but also other municipality departments such as the International Affairs Department, has further developed, guarded and carried out this international profile both for external and internal purposes.

From External to Internal Audiences: The Municipality View

Looking at the image building efforts of the municipality through the lens of self-portraiture reveals an internal struggle within the municipality with regard to their relation to the city's international image and their role as providers for citizens. Most academic analyses of The Hague's peace and justice image focus on its success with external, international audiences.[20] An 'indisputable' international image, in the words of the municipality's own branding strategy.[21] Contrastingly, the same strategic document states that the ultimate goal of the strategy is that every Hagenaar (inhabitant of The Hague) profits from the positive developments that the strategy achieves, for example in the areas of employment and city pride.[22] When proposed to the city council in 2015, it was also emphasized that the strategy *focuses* on the inclusion of inhabitants in the strategy.[23] But while

---

[18] Evert Meijers et al, "City Profile: The Hague," *Cities* 41 (2014): 97; Van der Wusten, "Legal Capital," 258.

[19] Van der Wusten, "Legal Capital," 262.

[20] Van der Wusten, "Legal Capital," 254–255; Schwöbel-Patel, *Marketing Global Justice.*

[21] The Hague Municipality, *Aanpak Haagse Citybranding 2020.* Doc. no. RIS288025. P. 5. https://denhaag.raadsinformatie.nl/document/3338671/1/RIS288025_bijlage%20Aanpak%20Haagse%20Citybranding%202020.

[22] 'Aanpak Haagse Citybranding 2020.'

[23] The Hague Municipality, 'Programma Internationaal'. 24 March 2014. Doc. no. RIS 288025_151208. https://denhaag.raadsinformatie.nl/document/3338664/1/155-17122015-RIS288025%20Aanpak%20Haagse%20Citybranding%202020.

the strategic document indeed repeatedly mentions the importance of the inhabitants, only very little is said about how this support will be achieved and how exactly local residents will benefit from the strategy. Our interview data suggests that the City of Peace and Justice image is approached and used differently by different departments within the municipality, with an alternating emphasis on its external, economic value or its social, internal meaning.[24] Strikingly, in our interviews with two key departments working with the Peace and Justice image—Bureau Citybranding and the International Affairs Department—a primarily external marketing rationale was firmly rejected in favour of a strong desire to build an image that serves The Hague's inhabitants. The views of these departments are further explored below.

A staff member of Bureau Citybranding explicitly notes that their work consists of much more than branding for economic purposes.[25] Instead of using the term marketing or branding, he prefers to describe the work of the bureau as developing and managing The Hague's 'positioning strategy'. The bureau aims to make visible the distinctive character of The Hague and to guard the consistent communication of this image. The interviewee emphasizes that this strategy goes beyond marketing, and he sees the bureau's branding efforts as a philosophy, more holistic than just a slogan. According to him, the core of the strategy is that the distinctive character of the city can 'do good' for its inhabitants. He notes that this function is often misunderstood when people hear the word city marketing or branding. Moreover, he signals that the 'City of Peace and Justice' story has been too elite-focused in the past. For the coming years, one of the bureau's main aims is to tell this story as simply as possible to make it accessible to the local inhabitants. The interviewee notes that the inhabitants of The Hague want a clear, small story. He refers to research that shows that people in The Hague value 'the human scale' and therefore many residents do not feel connected to the exaggerated story of the city's international achievements. In his view, big successes need to be made small if you want to reach the local audience. Furthermore, he notes that while 'city pride' is an important part of the strategy, The Hague currently

---

[24] For example, a tension between the The Hague municipality and the Ministry of Foreign Affairs, Hulleman and Govers, "The Hague," 154. Bureau Citybranding also emphasized a difference in approach between the municipality's economic department and the more socially oriented departments. Interview with authors, 21 April 2020.

[25] Interview with authors, 21 April 2020.

lags behind in this area. City pride of the inhabitants has long been side-lined by the municipality's prioritization of the city's economic developments. In the eyes of the Bureau, the city brand encompasses an ambition to improve city pride, internal liveability, economy and image of the city, for the benefit of its inhabitants. But the Bureau itself seems to be rather critical of the current achievements of the 'City of Peace and Justice' in this area.

A similar ambition to make the international image benefit the local is communicated by the municipality's International Affairs Department, whose main goal is to promote The Hague as City of Peace and Justice and to liaise with the international organizations it hosts. The inward-looking ambition of this department is currently mainly expressed through their explicit commitment to Sustainable Development Goal 16.3, which entails 'access to justice'. This goal is also translated into the concrete *access to law* (toegang tot recht) project, which took off in 2019 and is, at the time of writing, in its pilot phase. According to the policy officer, the rationale behind this initiative is for The Hague to 'practice what it preaches'.[26] The project focuses on the meaning of the 'City of Peace and Justice' label for the inhabitants of The Hague and aims to forge the connection between the international and the local. The idea is that if your international image is that of a justice provider, this should also be a key area of attention in the city itself. For this purpose, the municipality invited the NGO The Hague Institute for Innovation of Law (HiiL) to gather data from inhabitants about their experiences with access to law and justice. The project mainly focuses on three groups that potentially have difficulties in this area: women, residents with lower incomes and migrants. At the time of writing, there is not yet a clear picture of the outcomes of the survey, for its first phase of data collection has been delayed due to several bureaucratic and privacy issues. However, the initiation of this particular project is a clear indication of an interest in making the self-image beneficial to the inhabitants and a desire of the municipality to make the international relevant for the local.

A Scattered Self-Portrait

Increasing the stakes of local inhabitants in the city's international image corresponds with at least two functions of the self-portrait. In the approach

---

[26] Interview with authors, 26 March 2020.

of the *access to law* project, it translates into an ambition of the city to not only be the city of *international* peace and justice but to also be an exemplary 'just' city in the eyes and experiences of its inhabitants, making the image work for them. This resembles the aspect of self-portraiture as an act of self-reflection. Attempts to convey the value of The Hague's international character to local inhabitants and make them proud of this character moves into the other direction: it makes the inhabitants 'work' for the image. If inhabitants 'buy into' the image and adopt it as part of their identity and city pride, this is assumed to strengthen the communication of the desired image to external audiences.

While the ambition to build bridges between the outward 'City of Peace and Justice' brand and the interests of The Hague's own inhabitants is strongly emphasized, the municipality staff members we interviewed are quite aware of the difficulty of realizing this ambition. The Hague is one of the most segregated cities in the Netherlands.[27] It is therefore hardly possible to address The Hague's inhabitants as a homogenous group—ranging from expats to undocumented migrants—with a uniform relation to the City of Peace and Justice label. Some residents might not identify with the international brand; others may even have a diametrically opposed experience with their city's capacity to embody and distribute justice.[28] Also from an economical perspective the brand is not necessarily working for local residents. International organizations recruit worldwide and are not dependent on local labour market conditions,[29] which makes them potentially less interesting, important or visible for the local population. The city's efforts to interest and inform local audiences about the international institutions in their city that were mentioned in our interviews are International Open Day, The Hague Talks and meetings to bring 'old' locals in touch with 'new' locals (mainly expats). However, both Bureau Citybranding and the International Affairs Department recognize that it is quite possible that such events mainly draw the 'usual suspects', people who already feel the connection. In such a diverse city, it is a challenge to

[27] Meijers et al. "City Profile," 95; Robert Kloosterman and Hugo Priemus, "'The Hague a Dual City? Causes and Policy Responses," *Built Environment* 27, no. 3; Godfried Engbersen, Marion Van San and Arjen Leerkes, "A room with a view: Irregular immigrants in the legal capital of the world," *Ethnography* 7, no. 2 (2006).

[28] For example, Engbersen contrasts the way in which irregular migrants in The Hague are excluded from the welfare state with the city's 'legal capital of the world' profile. Engbersen et al, "A room with a view," 237.

[29] Meijers et al., "City Profile," 97.

make everyone 'belong to the The Hague family'[30] and to have all its members recognize themselves in a self-portrait that affiliates itself to international law.

HUMAN RIGHTS CITY AMSTERDAM

Amsterdam, the capital of the Netherlands, positions itself vis-à-vis the label 'Human Rights City'.[31] The municipality draws on the notion of Human Rights City in the construction of its self-image, even though Amsterdam is not a member of an official Human Rights City network, such as the People's Movement for Human Rights Learning or the European Human Rights Cities Network.[32] Amsterdam started to explicitly engage with human rights under the direction of mayor Van der Laan, who was a lawyer by training. During his terms, between 2010 and 2017, Amsterdam integrated human rights into several policy domains. Human rights were, for example, incorporated in the domain of children and youth,[33] in the policy for refugee integration, and in the policy for LGBTQ people.[34]

Human rights have not only shaped these particular policy domains, they have been shaping how Amsterdam sees itself. Even though Amsterdam does not refer to the Human Rights City in the activities of its city brand 'Iamsterdam', it does so through other channels. The International Office, which is committed to strengthening Amsterdam's international relations, and Program Diversity, which is committed to fostering social cohesion among the city's inhabitants, draw on the notion of Human Rights City. Our conversations with municipal staff of the International Office and Program Diversity show that Amsterdam's take

---

[30] Interview with authors, 21 April 2020.

[31] A human rights city is a city (local government, municipality) that explicitly refers to international or regional human rights treaties and uses human rights in their local policies, programmes and projects. There are several networks of human rights cities, but the term is often self-declared.

[32] The People's Movement for Human Rights Learning (PDHRE) is the first official Human Rights City network. See: https://www.pdhre.org/ and for the European network see: https://humanrightscities.net/.

[33] In the policy domain 'Youth' human rights are integrated because of new national youth law that is pillared on the International Convention on the Rights of the Child. City Council meeting on the Human Rights Agenda, 14 September 2016.

[34] For Amsterdam's policies on LGBTQ rights, see: https://www.amsterdam.nl/bestuur-organisatie/volg-beleid/diversiteit/lhbti-roze-agenda/.

on the Human Rights City is twofold: it is inward- and outward-looking at the same time. On the one hand, Amsterdam is already portraying itself as a Human Rights City for international audiences. On the other hand, the Human Rights City functions as an aspirational marker for an internal audience. Even within the confinement of a municipality, multiple, sometimes conflicting, self-images co-exist. In other words, Amsterdam depicts two selves: one of Amsterdam as a Human Rights City, and one of Amsterdam on the way to becoming one.

Amsterdam as a Human Rights City

The portrayal of Amsterdam as a Human Rights City is drafted by the International Office, for an international audience: the municipality's international partners, other cities, international organizations and corporations. Human rights have become an integral part of Amsterdam's foreign policy. Since 2009, Amsterdam's foreign policy has been presented under the slogan 'Amsterdam Responsible Capital'.[35] This slogan refers to Amsterdam's alleged responsibility abroad. As a 'responsible capital', Amsterdam, a relatively prosperous city, aims for reciprocity. It wants to help other cities in return for the economic benefits that result from the international relations.[36] Amsterdam wants to show solidarity, whilst profiting economically.[37] The portrayal as a Human Rights City helps to achieve both.

To give the reciprocity hands and feet, Amsterdam fosters cooperation on a number of policy terrains such as water management, economics, and citizenship and participation. In 2014, human rights were added to this list: 'considering the profile of Amsterdam and our role as Responsible Capital, and because human rights are more topical than ever, [they] must be integrated into the international policy'.[38] The integration of human rights in Amsterdam's foreign policies resulted in a number of practices:

---

[35] For the policy report on Amsterdam Responsible Capital, see Gemeente Amsterdam, *Internationaal Beleid 2014–2018. Amsterdam Internationaal Verantwoordelijke Hoofdstad*, https://assets.amsterdam.nl/publish/pages/869848/herijking_internationaal_beledi_20142018.pdf.

[36] Amsterdam Responsible Capital Policy Report, p. 4.

[37] Interview with the International Office, 2018.

[38] Amsterdam Responsible Capital Policy Report, p. 12.

the city shares its expertise on human rights,[39] it helps other organizations establish connections to human rights networks,[40] and the mayor of Amsterdam addresses human rights concerns during international visits with other governments.[41]

The Human Rights City also forms an essential part of the construction of Amsterdam's 'international profile'. When interacting with foreign organizations, governments and cities, Amsterdam profiles itself as a Human Rights City.[42] The International Office confirms this: 'when we [the International Office] give presentations, we state that we are a Human Rights City and that we strive for equality and equal opportunities'.[43] The portrayal of Amsterdam as a Human Rights City is not subject to strict rules, conditions or guidelines; the International Office portrays Amsterdam as a Human Rights City because it wants to be seen as such. The activities Amsterdam undertakes under the wing of 'Amsterdam Responsible Capital' emphasize the Human Rights City image. For example, by participating in the project Shelter City,[44] Amsterdam shows to the outside world that they care about human rights. This outward view is not a hidden intention; the municipality is explicit about this: 'With our participation in the [Shelter City] program the municipality of Amsterdam *shows* that they support the global fight for freedom and equality'.[45] According to the International Office, this international profile is crucial for the financial growth of Amsterdam. It is essential for attracting (EU) subsidies, and to be seen as a desirable location for foreign businesses. The

---

[39] Amsterdam predominantly focuses on sharing expertise on the following themes: the protection of human rights defenders, LGBTQ and women's rights. Amsterdam Responsible Capital Policy Report, p. 12.

[40] Amsterdam is a member of several human rights-oriented networks, such as Shelter City, Fearless Cities and Solidarity City initiative.

[41] Amsterdam Responsible Capital Policy Report, p. 15; see, for example, the following news articles that describe how mayor Van der Laan addressed the human rights situation in Israel: https://www.parool.nl/nieuws/van-der-laan-bespreekt-mensenrechten-in-israel~be5bff9c/.

[42] In a PowerPoint presentation that is used during international visits to introduce the city of Amsterdam, human rights form one of the focus points. See: https://www.amsterdam.nl/bestuur-organisatie/volg-beleid/internationale/presentation/.

[43] Interview with the International Office, 2018.

[44] Shelter City allows foreign human rights defenders to spend time in the Netherlands. See: https://sheltercity.nl/city/amsterdam/.

[45] Website Shelter City; website Program Diversity https://www.amsterdam.nl/bestuur-organisatie/volg-beleid/diversiteit/.

international profile facilitates acquisition. To some degree, the acquisition possibilities define to whom Amsterdam is responsible. The Responsible Capital Report describes that the geographical choices for foreign relations are also determined by their acquisition potential. Cooperation with cities that are located in what the International Office calls 'acquisition countries' is prioritized.[46]

To Become a Human Rights City

A few years later, in 2016, Amsterdam presented another approach to the Human Rights City. Program Diversity reasoned that Amsterdam needed to bring its local policies in line with its foreign policies: 'to take responsibility for human rights at other places, that is the easy part'.[47] As described, human rights were already a central theme of the work of the International Office, and were incorporated in several municipal domains, but there was no overarching and explicit human rights project dedicated to Amsterdam's internal affairs. This is (among other reasons) why the municipality launched the 'Amsterdam Human Rights Agenda'.[48] The Human Rights Agenda opens with a question: 'How do we, as a city, go about human rights?'[49] Approximately 300 inhabitants were asked to provide their personal view on human rights.[50] These views were assembled in a report, *Amsterdammers over Mensenrechten*, which was used as a basis for the Human Rights Agenda.[51] The Human Rights Agenda intends to concretize and translate human rights to the specific context of Amsterdam. It focuses on four priorities that were selected by the city's inhabitants: accessibility, children's rights, privacy and human rights education.

In the Human Rights Agenda, Amsterdam relates to the Human Rights City in a different way. The Human Rights City is aspirational; it is something to arrive at in the (near) future. The Human Rights Agenda,

---

[46] Amsterdam Responsible Capital Policy Report, p. 16.

[47] Interview with Program Diversity, 2018.

[48] The Amsterdam Human Rights Agenda can be found on the local government's webpage. Gemeente Amsterdam, *Brief Mensenrechten in Amsterdam*. See https://assets.amsterdam.nl/publish/pages/799393/brief_mensenrechten_in_amsterdam.pdf.

[49] Amsterdam Human Rights Agenda, p. 1.

[50] Interview with Program Diversity, 2018.

[51] For the report *Amsterdammers over Mensenrechten*, see: https://www.ohchr.org/Documents/Issues/LocalGvt/States/Amsterdam_5.pdf.

consequently, functions as an instrument to realize Amsterdam's Human Rights City aspirations.

This self-image, of Amsterdam on the way to becoming a human rights city, is adopted by another municipal department. Program Diversity is a small department that was tasked with developing the Human Rights Agenda. Besides the Human Rights Agenda, Program Diversity is responsible for projects on women's emancipation, inclusivity, polarization and radicalization, anti-discrimination and dialogue between different groups of inhabitants.[52] They have different aims and intended audiences than the International office. Where the International Office focuses on Amsterdam's interactions with cities, governments and organizations abroad, Program Diversity aims to reach all inhabitants of the city. Their desire is to create an inclusive city, regardless of Amsterdam's diverse character: 'Diversity is our strength. We do not focus on our differences, but on what brings us together [...] this is why the municipality's policy is not about diversity, it is about inclusivity'.[53] While the International Office states that Amsterdam is a human rights city already, Program Diversity questions this supposition. They conceive of the Human Rights City as something that is not easily achieved: 'perhaps we will be a real human rights city in 2, 3 or 4 years. We believe it is a slow process'.[54]

Program Diversity transposes this desire for an inclusive city to the Human Rights Agenda, and conceives of the Human Rights City as a marker that brings Amsterdam's diverse inhabitants together. The Human Rights Agenda, correspondingly, is inward-looking and portrays Amsterdam as a city that needs to work on human rights. More specifically, it encourages Amsterdam to assess their relation to human rights. Inhabitants and municipal staff are stirred to do so. Inhabitants are encouraged to strengthen their knowledge on human rights, because they are often not aware of what human rights stand for in the Netherlands. Additionally, human rights are presented as a 'common language' that can connect inhabitants, with different backgrounds, between themselves. Municipal staff, on the other hand, are urged to employ 'a human rights perspective' for their daily decision-making, because they often perceive

---

[52] See https://www.amsterdam.nl/bestuur-organisatie/volg-beleid/diversiteit/.
[53] See https://www.amsterdam.nl/bestuur-organisatie/volg-beleid/diversiteit/.
[54] Interview with Program Diversity, 2018.

human rights as something that is part of foreign policy, rather than as relevant for Amsterdam.[55]

A Portrait of Two Faces

The municipality of Amsterdam has not constructed a coherent self-portrait. On the contrary, the self-portrait is messy, and it consists of (at least) two selves: Amsterdam as a human rights city and Amsterdam as an aspiring human rights city. When two different local government departments act as makers, one may end up with different end-products. The International Office and Program Diversity have different intentions and audiences, which is why they have a dissimilar perception of the Human Rights City.

The self-portrait in which Amsterdam positions itself vis-à-vis the Human Rights City compels international audiences to see Amsterdam in a particular way, but it also makes Amsterdam look at itself. It incites self-reflection. Because Amsterdam was initially focusing on the outward side, it provoked a process of introspection, which led to the Human Rights Agenda. Program Diversity assessed the city's international 'human rights' self-image, which speaks to what branding literature suggests: the outward message needs to be in tune with the inward message for the self-image to be sincere.[56] However, because Program Diversity perceived that Amsterdam is not a 'real' Human Rights City yet, a more multifaceted portrait appeared. And as a consequence, Amsterdam's inward and outward messages are not in full harmony.

CONCLUSION

A self-portrait is never a realistic reflection of an objective reality. It shows an aspiration or desire for what one wishes to become or how one wishes to be seen by others. In the context of The Hague and Amsterdam, the self-portrait lens shows a plural, messy process rather than a uniform

[55] Interview with Program Diversity, 2018. This tendency is also explored by Barbara Oomen. See Barbara Oomen, "Rights for others: the slow home-coming of human rights in the Netherlands," in *Cambridge Studies in Law and Society*, ed. Christopher Arup, Martin Chanock and Pat O'Malley (Cambridge: Cambridge University Press, 2014).

[56] Paganoni, "City Branding and Social Inclusion in the Glocal City"; Stigel and Frimann, "City Branding – All Smoke, No Fire?"

strategy behind the desire to be or become an international law city. The international image is pursued because of several, at times competing, motives—for example, economic, social or reputational. The city self-portrait is made, used and reinterpreted continuously, by many different people with potentially diverging ideas about the portrait's primary tasks, responsibilities and audiences. Behind the international profile, brand or slogan, we have observed confusion about identity or even discomfort or frustration with certain labels or interpretations of the image. The image is always imperfect, sometimes too ambitious, and probably does not satisfy either side of the spectrum.

With the lens of the self-portrait we can revalue the city's image as a desire to portray oneself in a certain way to the outside world on the one hand, and an exercise in self-reflection on the other. In both The Hague and Amsterdam, the construction of an external international image seems to come first and the inward-looking considerations follow. The external communication is considered the 'easy part', leading the municipality to feel the need to 'practise what it preaches' internally, which can be seen as a form of introspection. Initiatives are undertaken to start living up to the expectations created by the city's international image, for it to transpire to its own inhabitants, such as the *access to law* project in The Hague or the educational efforts of the Amsterdam Human Rights Agenda.

We showed the struggle of the multiple makers of the self-portrait and their awareness of the possibility—or even probability—that the audience perceives it in different or unintended ways. Despite this awareness, both Amsterdam and The Hague show a persistent effort to affect the perception of the local population in favour of the international image. Considering these attempts of the municipality to increase the pride and knowledge of international law of its inhabitants, we may wonder if a self-portrait can or should enforce a change in its audience and adapt their way of seeing themselves in relation to the subject. And we may wonder to what extent the maker can affect this perception not only through making the portrait but also after the portrait is 'done'. As Cumming asks: 'when painted, has this self become someone independent of me?'[57] Is the city self-portrait starting to live its own life, independent of the initial strategy behind it? Based on this premature exploration of how municipal staff works with the image, we hypothesize that indeed the image lends itself to

---

[57] Cumming, "A Face to the World," 6.

many different interpretations and assumptions about its intended as well as its actual or desired aims.

In short, a coherent self-portrait in which self-reflection and external posture are perfectly aligned does not exist. Different timelines can merge as past, present and aspired future are represented at once. To stay with the fine arts, the international law city self-portrait is less a Rembrandt and more a late Picasso like his 'Buste d'homme Écrivant' that allows for multiple angles, perspectives and a mixture of styles to appear in one portrait.

BIBLIOGRAPHY

Anttiroiko, Ari-Veikko. 2015. City Branding as a Response to Global Intercity Competition. *Growth and Change* 46 (2): 233–252.

Aust, Helmut. 2015. Shining Cities on the Hill? The Global City, Climate Change, and International Law. *The European Journal of International Law* 26 (1): 255–278.

Blank, Yishai. 2006. The City and the World. *Columbia Journal of Transnational Law* 47 (686): 875–939.

Crozier, Ray, and Paul Greenhalgh. 1988. Self-Portraits as Presentations of Self. *Leonardo* 21 (1): 30.

Cumming, Laura. 2014. *A Face to the World: on Self-Portraits.* London: William Collins.

Engbersen, Godfried, Marion Van San, and Arjen Leerkes. 2006. A room with a view: Irregular immigrants in the legal capital of the world. *Ethnography* 7 (2): 209–242.

Hankinson, Graham, and Philippa Cowking. 1993. *Branding in Action: Cases and Strategies for Profitable Brand Management.* New York: McGraw-Hill.

Hulleman, Bengt Arne, and Robert Govers. 2011. The Hague, International City of Peace and Justice. In *City Branding*, ed. Keith Dinnie, 150–156. London: Palgrave Macmillan.

Jones, Amelia. 2002. The "Eternal Return": Self-Portrait Photography as a Technology of Embodiment. *Signs* 27 (4): 947–978.

Kavaratzis, Mihalis. 2004. From City Marketing to City Branding: Towards a Theoretical Framework for Developing City Brands. *Place Branding* 1 (1): 58–73.

Kavaratzis, Mihalis, and Gregory Ashworth. 2005. City Branding: An Effective Assertion of Identity or Transitory Marketing Trick? *Tijdschrift voor Economische en Sociale Geografie* 96 (5): 506–514.

Kloosterman, Robert, and Hugo Priemus. 2001. The Hague a Dual City? Causes and Policy Responses. *Built Environment* 27 (3): 167–175.

Meijers, Evert, et al. 2014. City Profile: The Hague. *Cities* 41: 97.

Nijman, Janne. 2016. Renaissance of the City as Global Actor. The Role of Foreign Policy and International Law Practices in the Construction of Cities as Global Actors. In *The Transformation of Foreign Policy: Drawing and Managing Boundaries from Antiquity to the Present*, ed. Gunther Hellmann, Andreas Fahrmeir, and Miloš Vec, 209–239. Oxford: Oxford Scholarship Online.

Oomen, Barbara. 2014. Rights for Others: The Slow Home-Coming of Human Rights in the Netherlands. In *Cambridge Studies in Law and Society*, ed. Christopher Arup, Martin Chanock, and Pat O'Malley. Cambridge: Cambridge University Press.

Oomen, Barbara, Martha F. Davis, and Michele Grigolo. 2016. Introduction: The Rise and Challenges of Human Rights Cities. In *Global Urban Justice: The Rise of Human Rights Cities*, ed. Barbara Oomen, Martha F. Davis, and Michele Grigolo, 1–22. Cambridge: Cambridge University Press.

Paganoni, Maria Cristina. 2012. City Branding and Social Inclusion in the Glocal City. *Mobilities* 7 (1): 13–31.

Schwöbel-Patel, Christine. 2021. *Marketing Global Justice: The Political Economy of International Criminal Law*. Cambridge: Cambridge University Press. Forthcoming.

Stigel, Jørgen, and Søren Frimann. 2006. City Branding—All Smoke, No Fire? *Nordicom Review* 2: 245–268.

van der Wusten, Herman. 2006. 'Legal Capital of the World': Political Centre-Formation in the Hague. *Tijdschrift voor Economische en Sociale Geografie* 97 (3): 253–266.

CHAPTER 6

International Legal Collage of an Ideal City

Miha Marčenko

INTRODUCTION

In international law and global governance, the city is becoming more and more visible as the crucial social and political frame through which international policies and norms can 'touch the ground' and influence how people around the world live.[1] Even more than that, through a network of

---

[1] Helmut Aust, "Shining Cities on the Hill? The Global City, Climate Change, and International Law" The European Journal of International Law 26, no.1 (2015); Helmut Aust and Anel Du Plessis, eds. *The Globalisation of Urban Governance: Legal perspectives on Sustainable development Goal 11.* New York: Routledge, 2019.; Helmut Aust and Janne Nijman, eds. *Research Handbook on Cities and International Law.* Cheltenham: Edward Elgar Publishing, forthcoming; Yishai Blank. "The City and the World" Columbia Journal of Transnational Law 44 (2006); Luis Eslava, *Local Space, Global Life: The Everyday Operation of International Law and Development.* Cambridge: Cambridge University Press, 2015.; Gerald Frug and David Barron. "International Local Government Law" The Urban lawyer 38, no. 1 (2006); Ileana M Porras. "The City and International Law: In Pursuit of Sustainable Development" Fordham Urban Law Journal 36 (2009); Miha Marčenko. "The Role of the city in international law and governance" PhD thesis, University of Amsterdam, The Netherlands, forthcoming; Janne Nijman. "Renaissance of the City as Global Actor" in *The*

M. Marčenko (✉)
T.M.C. Asser Instituut / University of Amsterdam, The Hague, The Netherlands
e-mail: M.Marcenko@asser.nl

© The Author(s), under exclusive license to Springer Nature
Switzerland AG 2020
S. Stolk, R. Vos (eds.), *International Law's Collected Stories*,
Palgrave Studies in International Relations,
https://doi.org/10.1007/978-3-030-58835-9_6

events and forums, international institutions, such as the UN, and a range of other actors engaged in international policy-making have been assembling ideas on what an ideal city based on norms and principles of international law should look like. Questions on how and by whom cities should be governed, and how they should fit into the global frame of governance, have been addressed by interweaving different international legal discourses such as the sustainable development agenda, international human rights law and economic liberalism.[2]

At the core of this international legal making of an ideal city has been a United Nations agency, the United Nations Human Settlements Programme, or UN-Habitat. UN-Habitat has been an actor encouraging a wider network of institutional actors to collectively develop a vision of an ideal city through the frame of which international legal goals and aspirations can be achieved.

The most prominent recent example of a UN-Habitat-led process that brought together a host of actors interested in the development of cities has been the HABITAT III conference held in 2016 in Quito, Ecuador.[3] At the end of the conference, a single document, the New Urban Agenda,[4] presented a definitive liberal vision of what an ideal city should look like and how it should be governed. The New Urban Agenda gives a vision of an ideal city based on sustainable development, economic liberalism, human rights, and good governance, among others.[5]

Transformation of Foreign Policy: Drawing and Managing Boundaries from Antiquity to the Present, edited by Gunther Hellmann, Andreas Fahrmeir, and Milo Vec, Oxford: Oxford University Press, 2016; Barbara Oomen and Moritz Baumgärtel. "Frontier Cities: The Rise of Local Authorities as an Opportunity for International Human Rights Law" The European Journal of International Law, 29, no. 2 (2018); Lisa Roodenburg. "Diversity and Migration in Global Cities: Human Rights as a Source of Trust and/or Control" PhD thesis, University of Amsterdam, The Netherlands, forthcoming.

[2] International law in this chapter overlaps with the concept of global governance. As such, international law does not signify only formal, state-centric institutional structure. Instead, it includes other less formal ways of international ordering that interact with and surround the norms, institutions and institutional processes considered to belong to the formal, state-centric, international institutional structure.

[3] "HABITAT III." HABITAT III. Last modified March 11 2020. http://habitat3.org/.

[4] UN General Assembly, *New Urban Agenda*, UNGA RES/71/256. New York, 2016.

[5] The New Urban Agenda is embedded in the long-lasting liberal governance agenda, promoted by the UN and other international institutions. See Ileana M Porras. "The City and International Law: In Pursuit of Sustainable Development" Fordham Urban Law Journal 36 (2009).

However, in this chapter I argue that it is problematic to view the shared (liberal) vision of a city as a cohesive creation that puts forward a linear normative narrative concerning global urbanization. Instead, by using the analytical lens of the collage, this chapter aims to more vividly present the tension and ambivalence that remain unresolved in international norm-and-policy-making related to cities and global urbanization.

Like the art of collage, the international legal image of an ideal city features ready-made discursive elements that, once assembled together, interrelate in a novel way but always also remain part of some other context. Moreover, the elements forming the collage of an ideal city do not seamlessly fit together. They remain in tension with one another and allow different interpretations of how an ideal city grounded in international law should look. Sustainable development goals, human rights norms, economic, environmental and other principles, as well as other elements, such as aspirations of municipal governments and civil society groups, are only roughly pasted together within the collage of the ideal city.

Additionally, it is the analytical lens of *collage-making* that offers a way to more vividly grasp the complexity of the process of international policy- and norm-making related to cities. Collage-making, usually done by one artist, can also be a collective art-making activity that allows for many hands to participate in the messy creation of the final piece—the collage. Through various forums, events, declarations and statements, UN-Habitat and a host of other actors try to make visible their particular visions of an ideal city, which prioritize certain values and visions.

This chapter thus engages with institutional processes within international law and global governance through which urban issues are discussed. It approaches the formation of the liberal urban agenda grounded in international law as a more erratic collage-making done by many hands, instead of a harmonious process led by one mind in many bodies, and visualizes the ambivalence of the making of an ideal city through international law.

The next section presents some forums through which a linear, international legal vision of a city is considered to be developed. The section after that proposes to view these same institutional processes through the analytical lenses of the collage and collage-making. It is through the lens of the collage that the tensions and complexities embedded in the international legal vision of an ideal city become more visible. More importantly, using the lens of the collage can help unveil and unsettle how the international legal processes focusing on urbanization favour or disfavour certain voices and ideas and silence others.

VISION OF AN IDEAL CITY

We live in an age in which the majority of the population lives in cities. Cities are places where 80 percent of the global economic activity takes place and where the majority of CO_2 emissions are produced. In addition, cities are spaces where the global inequality, poverty, homelessness and exclusion that define our times are entrenched.[6]

However, cities are also considered to be socio-political spaces that offer an opportunity to resolve social, environmental and economic problems. Due to the proximity of public and private actors, there arguably exists a potential in cities to rethink in a participatory manner how to develop novel local solutions to the problems plaguing our world, a potential that is not present on any other political scale.[7] As the previous UN Secretary General stated within the framework of sustainable development discourse, 'cities are places where the struggle for global sustainability will either be won or lost'.[8]

These words of the top UN official reflect a more extensive effort by the UN and other actors to create a commonly shared vision of future urban development. Or, as I argue, a vision of an ideal city built on shared values and principles of the global community that could and should be applied across the world.

At the centre of the United Nations' focus on cities stands UN-Habitat, an agency dedicated specifically to problems of urban governance and housing. The work of the agency at first focused primarily on programmes of slum upgrading in countries in the global South. However, over the years, UN-Habitat has started promoting wider policies on the sustainable

---

[6] UN Habitat, *World Cities Report 2016—Urbanization and Development: Emerging Futures.* Nairobi, 2016.

[7] Ibid. 47–68.

[8] "UN forum spotlights cities, where struggle for sustainability 'will be won or lost'" United Nations. Last modified July 14, 2018.

https://www.un.org/sustainabledevelopment/blog/2018/07/un-forum-spotlights-cities-struggle-sustainability-will-won-lost/.

management of urbanization.[9] It does not do this by itself, but rather by building platforms that encourage participatory thinking on the governance of cities.[10]

For example, World Urban Forums (WUF) taking place every two years bring together representatives of UN-Habitat and other international institutions, representatives of member-states, as well as representatives of transnational intercity organizations, NGOs, transnational community-based organizations and academics. Numbers of attendees are measured in tens of thousands.[11] At WUFs, the representatives of these institutional actors highlight the issues, which according to them impede the development of cities and the people living in them. Issues include environmental degradation, limited economic and social opportunities for youth and women, inequitable access to services, insufficient protection for human rights violations, poverty, health issues, and cultural issues.[12] Each WUF ends with an informal declaration that lays out a shared all-embracing vision of the future of global urban development (each WUF focuses on a specific theme, but otherwise promotes the same vision). Here is an example of this shared vision as worded in the Kuala Lumpur Declaration, accepted at the ninth WUF in 2018:

> we call for the deployment of all efforts, means and resources available towards the operationalization of the concept of cities for all, ensuring that all inhabitants, of present and future generations, without discrimination of any kind, are able to inhabit and produce just, safe, healthy, accessible, affordable, resilient and sustainable cities and human settlements to foster prosperity and quality of life for all.[13]

In the last two decades, the most visible attempt to create a cohesive vision of an ideal city was articulated in the New Urban Agenda (NUA), an informal UN declaration signed by many member-states.[14] The NUA

---

[9] UN Habitat, *World Cities Report 2016* (no.6).

[10] Prominent examples are World Urban Forums, described below, and a more long-lasting institutional process called the World Urban Campaign.

[11] "10th World Urban Forum in Abu Dhabi" UN-Habitat. Last modified May 10, 2020. https://wuf.unhabitat.org/sites/default/files/2020-02/WUF10_final_declared_actions.pdf.

[12] Ibid.

[13] UN-Habitat. World Urban Forum. *Kuala Lumpur Declaration on Cities 2030*. Kuala Lumpur, 2018.

[14] UN General Assembly, *New Urban Agenda*.

was accepted at the largest UN-led conference focused specifically on urban issues in recent history, HABITAT III. As the text of the NUA states at the beginning:

> We share a vision of cities for all, referring to the equal use and enjoyment of cities and human settlements, seeking to promote inclusivity and ensure that all inhabitants, of present and future generations, without discrimination of any kind, are able to inhabit and produce just, safe, healthy, accessible, affordable, resilient and sustainable cities and human settlements to foster prosperity and quality of life for all. [...] We aim to achieve cities and human settlements where all persons are able to enjoy equal rights and opportunities, as well as their fundamental freedoms, guided by the purposes and principles of the Charter of the United Nations, including full respect for international law.[15]

Even though the New Urban Agenda is a document that was formally created and accepted by states,[16] and HABITAT III was a state-centred conference, the institutional process encouraged input from other actors. Hundreds of thousands of people were involved in various stages of the conference.[17] At the conference itself, municipal governments and representatives of their intercity organizations, as well as representatives of various civil society organizations, were able to contribute their ideas.[18] More crucially, the preparatory discussions leading to the conference were designed in such a way as to allow representatives of states, municipal governments, civil society and academics to shape initial drafts of the New Urban Agenda together.[19]

HABITAT III and the World Urban Forums show the effort of the UN, and the wider network of actors, to create a shared global vision of

---

[15] Ibid, p. 12.

[16] The New Urban Agenda itself originates in Agenda 2030, a larger UN-led process aimed at creating a general blueprint for sustainable development. Through Agenda 2030, states have in 2015 agreed to try to accomplish 17 Sustainable Development Goals (SDGs). One of these goals, SDG 11, aims to make cities inclusive, safe, resilient and sustainable. See UN General Assembly, *Transforming our world: the 2030 Agenda for Sustainable Development*, A/RES/70/1 New York. 2015.

[17] "HABITAT III." HABITAT III. Last modified March 11 2020. http://habitat3.org/.

[18] "Habitat III Informal Hearings with Local Authorities Associations." IISD. Last modified October 9, 2018 http://enb.iisd.org/habitat/3/authorities/.

[19] "Policy units" HABITAT III. Last modified March 11 2020.
http://habitat3.org/the-new-urban-agenda/preparatory-process/policy-units/.

urban development, or in other words to create a vision of an ideal city based on international legal principles and norms. The ideal city is presented as a linear, clear 'work of art', the meaning and relevance of which is known to all who have taken part in creating it and who all approach it from a single point of view. It is thus an endeavour to construct a powerful simplified narrative that centres on the liberal interpretation of what an ideal city should look like. UN-Habitat states that in spite of national and local differences that have to be taken into account, the 'New Urban Agenda is universal in scope, participatory and people-centred; protects the planet; and has a long-term vision, …'.[20] In the NUA, the cities

> fulfil their social function, including the social and ecological function of land, with a view to progressively achieving the full realization of the right to adequate housing, … Are participatory, promote civic engagement, engender a sense of belonging and ownership among all their inhabitants, … Meet the challenges and opportunities of present and future sustained, inclusive and sustainable economic growth, leveraging urbanization for structural transformation, high productivity, value-added activities and resource efficiency.[21]

At first glance, the effort to create a shared vision of a city based on international law seems to have been successful. A pallet of actors has showed support to the UN-orchestrated vision seamlessly connecting principles of efficient governance, democratization, sustainable development, economic liberalism and international human rights law, as well as more specific visions such as the right to the city. Numerous UN member-states have accepted the (non-binding) NUA. The World Bank has been developing its urban financing mechanisms to support the goals contained in the NUA.[22] The largest intercity organization, United Cities and Local Governments (UCLG), representing thousands of municipal governments from all continents, has been deeply involved in the HABITAT III

---

[20] UN General Assembly, *New Urban Agenda*, p. 12.

[21] Ibid, pp. 12, 14.

[22] "Three big ideas to achieve sustainable cities and communities" World Bank. Last modified December 2018 http://www.worldbank.org/en/news/immersive-story/2018/01/31/3-big-ideas-to-achieve-sustainable-cities-and-communities. For more in-depth exploration of the World Bank's engagement with SDG 11 and New Urban Agenda see Judy L Baker, Gauri U. Gadgil. *East Asia and Pacific Cities: Expanding Opportunities for the Urban Poor*. World Bank: Washington, DC, 2017.

process and endorsed both the SDGs and NUA.[23] Additionally, on the side of the global civil society, Slum/Shack Dwellers International (SDI), which represents local groups of urban poor from over 700 informal settlements, has also participated in most of the forums and conferences led by UN-Habitat.[24] And these are only some examples out of hundreds if not thousands of institutional actors that have participated in the creation of the NUA and other declarations through which the liberal vision of an ideal city is articulated.

On the surface, then, the UN, resembling a conductor, has managed to bring together a network of actors representing cities, states, and international institutions and the civil society to develop a vision of an ideal city as a singular work of art that is shared by everyone. They seem to have crafted a vision of a city, grounded in international legal discourse, as a modernist work of art within which 'each aspect reinforces the effect of the others, creating an untroubled harmony'.[25]

Yet, instead of viewing the interaction of these various actors as resulting in a singular and linearly developed narrative, I propose to look at the development of a vision of an ideal city through international law more as an unpredictable art of collage-making.[26]

COLLAGE OF AN IDEAL CITY

Collage is a twentieth-century art form that has influenced painting, literature and other artistic fields. It is a form that allows the artist (the painter, the storyteller, etc.), or even a group of artists, to use ready-made elements in a novel context. In associating different contexts, collage-making enables a plurality of points of view on the same piece of art. Thus, instead of welcoming a singular, linear, narrative, the collage is an art form that

---

[23] Global Taskforce of Local and Regional Governments. *Statement of the second world assembly of local and regional governments to the third UN conference on housing and sustainable urban development.* Quito, 2016.

[24] Joel Bolnick, "Development as Reform and Counter-reform: Paths Travelled by Slum / Shack Dwellers International" in *Can NGOs make a difference? The challenge of development alternatives,* edited by Anthony Bebbington, Samuel Hickey, Diana Mitlin (2008 ZED Books), p. 331.

[25] Budd Hopkins. "Modernism and the Collage Aesthetic" New England Review 18, no. 2 (1997), p. 6.

[26] Thomas P. Brockelman, *The Frame and the Mirror: On Collage and the Postmodern.* Evanston: Northwestern University Press, 2001, p. 10.

leaves the tension between different elements unresolved and 'whose parts, seen together, metaphorically recreate the complex reality in which we actually live'.[27] Or, as the American literary critic Laszlo K. Gefin writes,

> Each ... element [of the collage] breaks the continuity or linearity of the discourse and leads necessarily to a double reading: that of the fragment perceived in the relation to its text of origin; that of the same fragment as incorporated into a new whole, a different totality.[28]

Looking at the example of the New Urban Agenda through the analytical lens of the collage puts the emphasis on the multiplicity of discourses and agendas contained within. These elements, while glued together in a single frame, fail to conceal the unresolved tensions between them. And using the analytical lens of collage-making shows the process of creating a vision of an ideal city made through international law not as a linear and harmonious activity, but instead as a precarious and messy process of collecting, cutting and pasting of various elements. As Rona Cran, the author of *Collage in Twentieth-Century Art, Literature, and Culture*, writes,

> Collage [is] about meaningful encounters and juxtapositions, about displacing, disrupting, and deconstructing, whilst simultaneously representing the possibility of dialogue and synthesis between heterogeneous elements.[29]

To visualize the complexity and ambivalence of the making of the vision of an ideal city through international law, one must bring out individual discursive elements of the vision of an ideal city and the contexts they are taken from.[30] To demonstrate this, the New Urban Agenda and the HABITAT III conference through which it was formulated serve as the focal point of this section.

---

[27] Budd Hopkins. "Modernism and the Collage Aesthetic" New England Review 18, no. 2 (1997), p. 9.

[28] Laszlo K. Gefin. "Collage Theory, Reception and the Cutups of William Burroughs" in *Perspectives on Contemporary Literature: Literature and the Other Arts*, edited by David Hershberg, Lexington: University Press of Kentucky, 1987, p. 94.

[29] Rona Cran, *Collage in Twentieth-Century art, literature, and Culture: Joseph Cornell, William Burroughs, Frank O'Hara, and Bob Dylan*. Farnham: Ashgate Publishing, 2014, p. 14.

[30] Ibid, p. 32.

The unavoidable starting point is that the New Urban Agenda is a document that can easily be read as reinforcing a state-centric and sovereignty-based view on what cities and urban development mean.

> We, Heads of State and Government, Ministers and High Representatives, [...] Recognize the leading role of national Governments [...] in the definition and implementation of inclusive and effective urban policies and legislation for sustainable urban development[.][31]

The city in the state-centric context is understood as a subdivision of the state, a local socio-political space and unit of governance through which policies and norms created by nation-state authorities are localized. The NUA can thus be read as envisioning the city as an entity through which the state is able to achieve sustainable development.

In contrast to the view of the states, United Cities and Local Governments (UCLG), the organization that represents the interests of municipal governments, envisions an ideal city as a more autonomous governance frame. The city is envisioned as a decentralized governance entity, with the municipal government at the centre, which is integrated into global governance mechanisms and bound by human rights and principles of sustainable development.[32] The UCLG's reading of the NUA celebrates the emphasis placed on decentralization and subsidiarity as principles crucial for sustainable development. Furthermore, it also celebrates the commitment articulated in the NUA to strengthen the capacities of local governments, to implement effective multi-level governance mechanisms and to support decentralized city-to-city cooperation.[33] UCLG's vision of an ideal city is therefore based on very different organizational principles than the one envisioned by states. It is a vision of a city governed by the municipal government which functions through the mechanisms of multi-level governance.

The World Bank, the institution that leads the financing of urban development, approaches the vision of an ideal city very differently. The urban

---

[31] UN General Assembly, *New Urban Agenda*. para 15.

[32] United Cities and Local Governments. *GOLD IV Report: Decentralization and Local Democracy in the World*. Barcelona, 2017.

[33] "The II World Forum of Local Governments showcases local policies committed to 2030 Agenda." United Cities and Local Governments. Last modified January 25 2019. https://www.uclg.org/en/media/news/ii-world-forum-local-governments-showcases-local-policies-committed-2030-agenda.

funding that the World Bank offers around the world always comes attached with directions on how to make cities more productive, competitive, profitable and attractive to local, regional and global private investment.[34] According to the World Bank, all of this then leads to more prosperous, liveable and resilient and sustainable cities.[35]

The sustainability and prosperity of cities for the Bank hinges on a governing environment that attracts private investments and enables growth of urban markets. This is part of the World Bank's vision of eradication of poverty around the world, which is to be achieved through economic development, growth and economic liberalization. In other words, if the capitalist economy in cities is growing, if private investors are satisfied, then the city can be profitable and thus prosperous for all inhabitants.[36] It could be said that the ideal city for the World Bank is therefore a prosperous and productive capitalist city within the global capitalist system. Since a large part of the New Urban Agenda is dedicated to economic sustainability, it could be argued that the ideas that the World Bank stands for have become part of the collage of an ideal city.[37]

Furthermore, for Slum Dwellers International (SDI), an organization representing slum dwellers, an ideal city again means something very different. Their vision is to develop a city that is more egalitarian and is co-produced by the poorest city dwellers who are too often made illegal, unwelcome and invisible. Their ideal city is built through participatory governance, where slum dwellers co-manage their settlements and neighbourhoods.[38] The ideal city for SDI is thus one that leaves no one behind.

---

[34] "How do city leaders get things done? Learning from mayors in Japan." World Bank. Last modified December 11, 2018. http://blogs.worldbank.org/sustainablecities/category/tags/new-urban-agenda.

[35] World Bank. *Africa's Cities: Opening Doors to the World*. by Somik Vinay Lall, Vernon Henderson and Anthony J Venables. Washington DC, 2017, pp. 8–32; World Bank. *Competitive cities for jobs and growth: what, who, and how*. Austin Kilroy, Louis Francis, Megha Mukim, Stefano Negri. Washington, D.C, 2015.

[36] World Bank. *Africa's Cities: Opening Doors to the World*, by Somik Vinay Lall, Vernon Henderson and Anthony J Venables. Washington DC, 2017.

[37] UN General Assembly, *New Urban Agenda*, pp. 21–24.

[38] "Slum Dwellers International joins the World Urban Campaign." Muungano. Last modified December 2018. https://www.muungano.net/browseblogs/2013/04/30/slum-dwellers-international-joins-the-world-urban-campaign.

Their vision of an ideal city based on participatory governance-from-below is also part of the NUA.[39]

A similar participatory vision of urban governance that has also found its way into the NUA is articulated through the concept of the right to the city.[40] This right is a rallying cry used by many civil society actors who envision cities to be understood as a public good. As stated by the Global Platform for the Right to the City, which gathers numerous actors interested in urban development:

> The Right to the City is the outcome of decades of collective and bottom-up creation that epitomizes a new paradigm providing an alternative framework to re-think cities on the basis of the principles of social justice, equity, democracy and sustainability.[41]

Linked to human rights initiatives, the Right to the City represents an alternative to many other visions of the ideal city that found a place in the NUA. In the words of the Global Platform for the Right to the City:

> Some countries, especially the most developed ones, were against this vision of city as a common good, because is exactly the opposite of competitive cities, exactly the opposite of smart cities, exactly the opposite of the cities as a business. We don't want only the social function of the land, but also the social function of the city.[42]

This tension between different visions of an ideal city can also be seen in the different approaches taken by UN agencies. For example, the UN Special Rapporteur for the Right to Adequate housing envisions the ideal city as a governance frame that protects and promotes human rights and, more specifically, the right to adequate housing.[43] The Right to Adequate

---

[39] Slum Dwellers International. *Know Your City: Slum Dwellers Count.* Cape Town, 2018, p. 2.

[40] David Harvey. "The Right to the City." New Left Review, Vol 53 (2008), pp. 23–40.

[41] "Habitat3: celebrate the inclusion of The Right to the City in the New Urban Agenda" Global Platform for the Right to the City. Last modified January 2019 http://www.right-tothecityplatform.org.br/habitat3-celebrate-the-inclusion-of-the-right-to-the-city-in-the-new-urban-agenda/.

[42] Ibid.

[43] UN General Assembly. *Report of the Special Rapporteur on adequate housing as a component of the right to an adequate standard of living, and on the right to non-discrimination in this context.* A/70/270. New York 2015; UN General Assembly. *Report of the Special*

Housing is included in the New Urban Agenda and the Special Rapporteur has been part of all of UN-Habitat's processes. Yet, right before the HABITAT III conference, Special Rapporteurs working at the UN Office of the High Commissioner for Human Rights collectively issued a warning that the New Urban Agenda is not human rights-centred enough.[44]

This warning issued by Special Rapporteurs can also be seen as a criticism of a vision of an ideal city articulated through sustainable development discourse, a discourse that has in other contexts also been accused of masking political decisions behind the language of science of governing based on scientifically supported indicators and targets that lead to managerialism and technocracy.[45] In such a way, UN-Habitat's vision of an ideal city grounded in the sustainable development agenda, in spite of it being presented as a universal frame, also reveals itself to be just one element in the collage.

This was also visible at the HABITAT III conference, where alternative, informal, forums were held in opposition to the main event. There, more radical voices belonging to the global civil society showed their opposition to the vision of the ideal city promoted by the UN. Even though the right to the city, one of the concepts used as a rallying cry in these alternative forums, has been incorporated in the NUA, the voices that have been shut out claim its meaning has been completely watered down.[46]

All of these different discourses, voices and visions used in international urban governance show that the unitary image of an ideal city is a mirage.[47] The vision of an ideal city grounded in international law is better seen as a

---

Rapporteur on adequate housing as a component of the right to an adequate standard of living, and on the right to non-discrimination in this context. A/HRC/28/62 New York 2014.

[44] "Open statement Habitat III: Shift towards a New Urban Agenda based on human rights." UN Office of the High Commissioner for Human Rights. Last modified January 2019. https://www.ohchr.org/EN/NewsEvents/Pages/DisplayNews.aspx?NewsID= 20669&LangID=E.

[45] Jane Briant Carant "Unheard voices: a critical discourse analysis of the Millennium Development Goals' evolution into the Sustainable Development Goals" Third World Quarterly 38, no. 1 (2017), pp. 16–41; Sanjay Reddy and Antoine Heuty, "Global Development Goals: The Folly of Technocratic Pretensions." Development Policy Review 26 no. 1 (2008), pp. 5–28.

[46] "Alternative Forums outside of Habitat III" Habitat International Coalition. Last modified January 2018. http://www.hlrn.org/news.php?id=pnFpZw==#.XKnuX5gzbb3.

[47] For a different view see: David Satterthwaite, "Successful, safe and sustainable cities: towards a New Urban Agenda" Commonwealth Journal of Local Governance 19 (2016), p. 8.

collage of ready-made elements precariously assembled together to give a sense of direction to the global urban governance. Therefore, the vision of an ideal city is a collage which remains in the making and 'call[s] attention to the irreducible heterogeneity of the "postmodern condition"' in which international law is produced.[48] Within the international legal vision of an ideal city, one finds visions of a sustainable city, of a city of human rights, of a city as public good, of a city as a commodity, and of a city as a growth machine. Additionally, there are visions of a city as an autonomous frame of governance, a city as nothing more than part of the state, and also a city as a local unit of multi-level global governance.

Using the lens of collage-making thus destabilizes the narrative that the process of creation of an international legal vision of an ideal city has been harmonious and has somehow ended in consensus. Instead, the effort to construct a linear, conclusive narrative is a political choice that attempts to disguise the continuing unresolved tensions among the plurality of visions of an ideal city.

Thus, by showing the unstable nature and multiple interpretations and meanings of the international legal vision of an ideal city, the analytical lens of the collage disrupts the illusion of a consensual harmonious approach to global urban development.[49] In a world in which the growth of urban homelessness and slums is continuing unabated,[50] the disruption of the status quo offered by the lens of the collage is a first step towards a necessarily more visible political conflict over cities and their place in international law and global governance. Or in the words of Chantal Mouffe:

> Instead of trying to erase the traces of power and exclusion, democratic politics requires us to bring them to the fore, to make them visible so that they can enter the terrain of contestation. And the fact that this must be envisaged as an unending process should not be cause for despair because the desire to reach a final destination can only lead to the elimination of the political and to the destruction of democracy. In a democratic polity,

[48] Thomas P. Brockelman. *The Frame and the Mirror: On Collage and the Postmodern.* Evanston: Northwestern University Press, 2001, p. 10.

[49] Kathleen Vaughan. "Pieced Together: Collage as an Artist's Method for Interdisciplinary Research." International Journal of Qualitative Methods 4, no.1 (2005), p. 32.

[50] UN Habitat, *World Cities Report 2016—Urbanization and Development: Emerging Futures.* Nairobi, 2016, pp. 47–68; UN General Assembly. *Report of the Special Rapporteur on adequate housing as a component of the right to an adequate standard of living, and on the right to non-discrimination in this context.* A/HRC/34/5118. New York, 2017.

conflicts and confrontations, far from being a sign of imperfection, indicate that democracy is alive and inhabited by pluralism.[51]

CONCLUSION

This chapter has shown that a vision of an ideal city has been developing through international law and global governance, a vision of an ideal city based on the principles and goals of the sustainable development agenda, international human rights law, economic liberalism, and other specific discourses such as the right to the city. These different elements have been presented as the building blocks of a consensual and harmonious international legal vision of an ideal city, a vision that has been created through UN-led institutional processes such as World Urban Forums and especially through the HABITAT III conference. Through these processes a network of institutional actors is claimed to have come to a shared understanding of the direction of global urban development.

Yet, I have argued that the image of an ideal city created through international law should instead be looked at through the analytical lens of the collage. The lens of the collage makes visible individual discursive elements out of which the international legal vision of an ideal city is assembled. These elements, representing specific visions of an ideal city, are only roughly pasted together and remain in tension with one another. Moreover, using the analytical lens of collage-making shows that the process of developing a vision of an ideal city through international law is contentious. Therefore, using the analytical lenses of the collage and collage-making offers a way of disrupting any linear narratives on what the urban future should look like. Approaching the international legal vision of an ideal city as a collage offers the first step to unsettling the political status quo that leaves the entrenched exclusionary practices of urban development intact.

BIBLIOGRAPHY

BOOKS AND ARTICLES

Aust, Helmut. 2015. Shining Cities on the Hill? The Global City, Climate Change, and International Law. *The European Journal of International Law* 26: 1.

---

[51] Chantal Mouffe. *The Democratic Paradox.* New York: Verso, 2000, p. 33.

Aust, Helmut, and Anel Du Plessis, eds. 2019. *The Globalisation of Urban Governance: Legal perspectives on Sustainable development Goal 11*. New York: Routledge.

Aust, Helmut, and Janne Nijman, eds. Forthcoming. *Research Handbook on Cities and International Law*. Cheltenham: Edward Elgar Publishing.

Baker, Judy L., and Gauri U. Gadgil. 2017. *East Asia and Pacific Cities: Expanding Opportunities for the Urban Poor*. Washington, DC: World Bank.

Blank, Yishai. 2006. The City and the World. *Columbia Journal of Transnational Law* 44.

Bolnick, Joel. 2008. Development as Reform and Counter-reform: Paths Travelled by Slum / Shack Dwellers International. In *Can NGOs Make a Difference? The Challenge of Development Alternatives*, ed. Anthony Bebbington, Samuel Hickey, and Diana Mitlin. London: ZED Books.

Briant Carant, Jane. 2017. Unheard Voices: A Critical Discourse Analysis of the Millennium Development Goals' Evolution into the Sustainable Development Goals. *Third World Quarterly* 38 (1).

Brockelman, Thomas P. 2001. *The Frame and the Mirror: On Collage and the Postmodern*. Evanston: Northwestern University Press.

Cran, Rona. 2014. *Collage in Twentieth-Century Art, Literature, and Culture: Joseph Cornell, William Burroughs, Frank O'Hara, and Bob Dylan*. Farnham: Ashgate Publishing.

Eslava, Luis. 2015. *Local Space, Global Life: The Everyday Operation of International Law and Development*. Cambridge: Cambridge University Press.

Frug, Gerald, and David Barron. 2006. International Local Government Law. *The Urban Lawyer* 38 (1).

Gefin, Laszlo K. 1987. Collage Theory, Reception and the Cutups of William Burroughs. In *Perspectives on Contemporary Literature: Literature and the Other Arts*, ed. David Hershberg. Lexington: University Press of Kentucky.

Harvey, David. 2008. The Right to the City. *New Left Review* 53.

Hopkins, Budd. 1997. Modernism and the Collage Aesthetic. *New England Review* 18 (2).

Marčenko, Miha. Forthcoming. *The Role of the City in International Law and Governance*. PhD thesis, University of Amsterdam, The Netherlands.

Mouffe, Chantal. 2000. *The Democratic Paradox*. New York: Verso.

Nijman, Janne. 2016. Renaissance of the City as Global Actor. In *The Transformation of Foreign Policy: Drawing and Managing Boundaries from Antiquity to the Present*, ed. Gunther Hellmann, Andreas Fahrmeir, and Milo Vec. Oxford: Oxford University Press.

Oomen, Barbara, and Moritz Baumgärtel. 2018. Frontier Cities: The Rise of Local Authorities as an Opportunity for International Human Rights Law. *The European Journal of International Law* 29 (2).

Porras, Ileana M. 2009. The City and International Law: In Pursuit of Sustainable Development. *Fordham Urban Law Journal* 36.

Reddy, Sanjay, and Antoine Heuty. 2008. Global Development Goals: The Folly of Technocratic Pretensions. *Development and Policy Review* 26 (1).

Roodenburg, Lisa. Forthcoming. *Diversity and Migration in Global Cities: Human Rights as a Source of Trust and/or Control.* PhD thesis, University of Amsterdam, The Netherlands.

Satterthwaite, David. 2016. Successful, Safe and Sustainable Cities: Towards a New Urban Agenda. *Commonwealth Journal of Local Governance* 19.

Vaughan, Kathleen. 2005. Pieced Together: Collage as an Artist's Method for Interdisciplinary Research. *International Journal of Qualitative Methods* 4 (1).

WEBSITES

10th World Urban Forum in Abu Dhabi. UN-Habitat. Last modified May 10, 2020. https://wuf.unhabitat.org/sites/default/files/2020-02/WUF10_final_declared_actions.pdf.

Alternative Forums Outside of Habitat III. Habitat International Coalition. Last modified January 2018. http://www.hlrn.org/news.php?id=pnFpZw==#.XKnuX5gzbb3.

HABITAT III. Last modified March 11, 2020. http://habitat3.org/.

Habitat III Informal Hearings with Local Authorities Associations. IISD. Last modified October 9, 2018. http://enb.iisd.org/habitat/3/authorities/.

Habitat3: Celebrate the Inclusion of The Right to the City in the New Urban Agenda. Global Platform for the Right to the City. Last modified January 2019. http://www.righttothecityplatform.org.br/habitat3-celebrate-the-inclusion-of-the-right-to-the-city-in-the-new-urban-agenda/.

How Do City Leaders Get Things Done? Learning from Mayors in Japan. World Bank. Last modified December 11, 2018. http://blogs.worldbank.org/sustainablecities/category/tags/new-urban-agenda.

Open Statement Habitat III: Shift towards a New Urban Agenda Based on Human Rights. UN Office of the High Commissioner for Human Rights. Last modified January 2019. https://www.ohchr.org/EN/NewsEvents/Pages/DisplayNews.aspx?NewsID=20669&LangID=E.

Policy Units. HABITAT III. Last modified March 11, 2020. http://habitat3.org/the-new-urban-agenda/preparatory-process/policy-units/.

Slum Dwellers International Joins the World Urban Campaign. Muungano. Last modified December 2018. https://www.muungano.net/browseblogs/2013/04/30/slum-dwellers-international-joins-the-world-urban-campaign.

The II World Forum of Local Governments Showcases Local Policies Committed to 2030 Agenda. United Cities and Local Governments. Last modified January 25, 2019. https://www.uclg.org/en/media/news/ii-world-forum-local-governments-showcases-local-policies-committed-2030-agenda.

Three Big Ideas to Achieve Sustainable Cities and Communities. World Bank. Last modified December 2018. http://www.worldbank.org/en/news/immersive-story/2018/01/31/3-big-ideas-to-achieve-sustainable-cities-and-communities.

UN Forum Spotlights Cities, Where Struggle for Sustainability 'Will Be Won or Lost'. United Nations. Last modified July 14, 2018. https://www.un.org/sustainabledevelopment/blog/2018/07/un-forum-spotlights-cities-struggle-sustainability-will-won-lost/.

DOCUMENTS AND PUBLICATIONS

Global Taskforce of Local and Regional Governments. 2016. *Statement of the Second World Assembly of Local and Regional Governments to the Third UN Conference on Housing and Sustainable Urban Development.* Quito.

Slum Dwellers International. 2018. *Know Your City: Slum Dwellers Count,* 2. Cape Town.

UN General Assembly. 2014. *Report of the Special Rapporteur on Adequate Housing as a Component of the Right to an Adequate Standard of Living, and on the Right to Non-Discrimination in this Context.* A/HRC/28/62, New York.

———. 2015a. *Report of the Special Rapporteur on Adequate Housing as a Component of the Right to an Adequate Standard of Living, and on the Right to Non-Discrimination in this Context.* A/70/270, New York.

———. 2015b. *Transforming Our World: The 2030 Agenda for Sustainable Development.* A/RES/70/1, New York.

———. 2016. *New Urban Agenda.* UNGA RES/71/256, New York.

———. 2017. *Report of the Special Rapporteur on Adequate Housing as a Component of the Right to an Adequate Standard of Living, and on the Right to Non-Discrimination in this Context.* A/HRC/34/5118, New York.

UN-Habitat. 2016. *World Cities Report 2016—Urbanization and Development: Emerging Futures.* Nairobi.

UN-Habitat. World Urban Forum. 2018. *Kuala Lumpur Declaration on Cities 2030.* Kuala Lumpur.

United Cities and Local Governments. 2017. *GOLD IV Report: Decentralization and Local Democracy in the World.* Barcelona.

World Bank. 2015. *Competitive Cities for Jobs and Growth: What, Who, and How.* Austin Kilroy, Louis Francis, Megha Mukim, and Stefano Negri. Washington, DC.

———. 2017. *Africa's Cities: Opening Doors to the World,* by Somik Vinay Lall, Vernon Henderson, and Anthony J Venables. Washington, DC.

CHAPTER 7

The Museum of White Terror, Taipei: 'Children, don't talk politics'

Renske Vos and Owen Zong-Syuan Han

The Jing-Mei White Terror Memorial Park and its accompanying National Human Rights Museum in Taipei are the site of the former Xindian military prison[1] and military court for political dissidents, in use during the period of 'White Terror' which marked Taiwan for over 40 years and lasted until the early 1990s.[2] We visited this former prison now turned museum as part of the course Transnational Law taught at National Taiwan University (NTU) in the final days of the winter of 2020. As a class we set out to see how we could connect the story of the museum to the theme of

---

[1] See: 'Xindian Military Prison', 'Historical Sites of injustice', National Human Rights Museum, visited 22 May 2020, https://hsi.nhrm.gov.tw/home/en-us/injusticelandmarks-en.

[2] 'Info', National Human Rights Museum, visited 22 May 2020, https://www.nhrm.gov.tw/en/.

R. Vos (✉)
VU Amsterdam, Amsterdam, The Netherlands
e-mail: r.n.vos@vu.nl

O. Z.-S. Han
National Taiwan University, Taipei, Taiwan
e-mail: r07a21100@ntu.edu.tw

S. Stolk, R. Vos (eds.), *International Law's Collected Stories*,
Palgrave Studies in International Relations,
https://doi.org/10.1007/978-3-030-58835-9_7

115

our course: Would it be possible to view this museum as a transnational legal actor of sorts? And what, if anything, could this museum show or tell, that international law cannot? From the reflections this visit evoked, we pick up on one in particular: where the international legal status of Taiwan remains uncertain, we view the story of this museum as a plea for Taiwanese sovereignty and ultimately independence.

The literary genre this chapter seeks to engage with is that of the museum, and specifically the museum guided tour.[3] We view the guided tour as a moment of encounter in which the museum presents its carefully designed story, and we as a group of students can 'absorb the story, but also ignore it, misunderstand it, criticize it, or be distracted by the surroundings'.[4] The object here is 'to pause to reflect on what it means to find ourselves in this encounter'.[5] This exercise is situated explicitly within the research project Legal Sightseeing,[6] which opens up from a sense of wonder at the spectacular yet trivial manifestation of international law in encounters with a plurality of audiences in the usual as well as unexpected places, such as in 'the school trip to the human rights museum'. The question posed by the research project is: What is international law doing here? In the context of this visit to the White Terror museum, we use this question to ask what lights up for us when we bring international law to this encounter.

We encounter the museum and specifically this guided tour as a group of relatively informed visitors, with some more informed than others on the subjects of human rights and Taiwanese history. Beforehand we, as teacher and teaching assistant, spoke with the students about how their participation would be input for this chapter, and they were invited to co-create it. Up front, the brief was to look around, to see what would stand out, to notice details.[7] Students were asked to take photographs during

---

[3] Taking inspiration from the fields of museum studies, transitional justice, memory law, and (dark) tourism, see, for example, Joyce Apsel, *Introducing Peace Museums* (London: Routledge, 2016); Janine Clark, "Reconciliation through Remembrance? War Memorials and the Victims of Vukovar," *International Journal of Transitional Justice* 7 (2013): 116; Ulad Belavusau and Aleksandra Gliszczyńska-Grabias (eds.), *Memory: Towards Legal Governance of History* (Cambridge: CUP, 2017); John Lennon and Malcolm Foley, *Dark Tourism: The Attraction of Death and Disaster* (London: Thomson, 2000).

[4] Sofia Stolk and Renske Vos, "International Legal Sightseeing: *Leiden Journal of International Law* 33, no. 1 (2020): 1.

[5] Ibid. at 3.

[6] About the research project: www.legalsightseeing.org.

[7] For methodological inspiration see: Debbie Lisle and Heather Johnson, "Lost in the aftermath," *Security Dialogue* 50 no. 1 (2018): 20–39.

the tour, and to select one photo that they felt captured their visit and that they would discuss afterwards. Following the discussion, they would write down their thoughts in a short reflection, producing a postcard to accompany their picture.[8] We posed a sequence of three questions: What do you see in the photograph? What does that mean to you? How can you connect this to transnational law? Holding these questions in our mind and note cards in our hands, we set out on our museum tour.

As students of international law, it is as much us who bring the law along as it is the museum's doing in calling on human rights. Moreover, our lens is wider than the museum's focus on human rights. This broader lens allows for a meta-perspective on the narrative that the museum presents. Though the museum itself does not mention the question of Taiwan's independence, our perspective makes visible the possibility of the museum's taking ownership of Taiwan's past as a means of establishing Taiwan's sovereignty and independent place in the world. This argument gains strength in light of the support that the Taiwanese government has given to the opening of the National Human Rights Museum. We interpret this support as all the more significant in light of competing views of Taiwan's history and future that the two rival political parties seek to advance, as we will explore towards the end of the chapter.[9]

In this chapter we contend that because of the uncertainty that persists under international law as to Taiwan's independent status, other means of establishing an international rapport and of fostering international support are sought and advocated by the current government. Where formal diplomacy is not possible due to Taiwan's status, creative alternatives are pursued.[10] The museum as popular with school visits and as a loved

---

[8] For students' photos and reflections see: "The Museum of White Terror, Taipei," *legal sightseeing*, https://legalsightseeing.org/2020/05/26/white-terror/.

[9] See 陳齊奐(Qi-Huan Tan), "景美人權文化園區的導覽敘事與人權教育初探 [Study on the Narrative Structure and Human Rights Education of the Jing-Mei Human Rights Memorial and Cultural Park]," *Museology Quarterly*, 28, no 3 (July 2014): 87–110, https://doi.org/10.6686/MuseQ.201407_28(3).0006.

[10] Such as a '[Face]Mask Diplomacy' following the global COVID-19 outbreak, Nicole Jao, "'Mask Diplomacy' a Boost for Taiwan," *Foreign Policy*, 13 April 2020, accessed 22 May 2020, https://foreignpolicy.com/2020/04/13/taiwan-coronavirus-pandemic-mask-soft-power-diplomacy/; Hsin-yu Wang and Joseph Yeh, 'Crowdfunded 'Taiwan can help' ad published in New York Times', *Focus Taiwan* (CNA English News), 14 April 2020, accessed 25 May 2020.

destination of tourists from Taiwan and abroad[11] is a space to present Taiwan as a progressive democracy, worthy of inclusion in the international community of States, with and through the first human rights museum in Asia.

'Walking into the Memory of White Terror'[12]

A group of us huddled together under cover of the Law Faculty entrance as it rained heavily on the morning of our visit. We had opted to travel to the museum together by bus and laughed as we alighted at the sensation of a true 'school trip'. Some more students knew the way and joined us at the museum directly. We were now a group of 15, a mix of Taiwanese and foreign exchange students, their teacher and teaching assistant. Those who were not from Taiwan originated from Singapore, Indonesia, Japan, Germany, France, Spain, Sweden, and the Netherlands. This was our last of six classes together, taken over the course of two weeks as an intensive course.

There were no other visitors at the museum during our time there. This could have been due to the poor weather, the early hour, or self-precautions related to Covid-19. As the rain came down around us, one of the students remarked how visiting this place in bright sunshine would be more eerie still.

Before our guided tour we were shown a video to introduce the museum.[13] 'Recalling the past and looking into the future', it began. A Taiwanese student later noted the significance of this moment to her: 'when watching the video clip together, it's interesting to find out foreigners are interested and willing to know what happened. The similar feelings we hold toward the tragic event makes me feel kind of warm'.[14]

---

[11] For the ambiguities involved in simultaneously communicating legal values to an internal and external audience, see Roodenburg and Stolk in this volume. Specifically for the Taiwanese context: Anya Bernstein, "The Social Life of Regulation in Taipei City Hall: The Role of Legality in the Administrative Bureaucracy," *Law & Social Inquiry* 33, no. 4 (2008): 925.

[12] Jing-Mei White Terror Memorial Park, information booklet (on file with authors).

[13] "國家人權博物館白色恐怖景美紀念園區簡介 [Introduction to the White Horror Jingmei Memorial Park of the National Museum of Human Rights (EN)]," video zone, National Museum of Human Rights, accessed 24 March 2020, https://www.nhrm.gov.tw/en/movie_85_3874.html.

[14] Student written reflection, on file with authors.

Fig. 7.1 Students gathered around the tour guide. (Photo: Renske Vos)

After the video screening, we set out with the tour guide. All of us were given headphones tuned to our guide's microphone, so that she would not have to raise her voice over the sound of the rain. This also allowed us to walk around quite freely, whilst still being able to hear the tour narrative. Students responded by listening to the tour attentively, reading information signs and asking questions, but also and perhaps mostly by carefully observing the spaces and displays, looking around, and taking photographs—though taking photographs was of course also part of their assignment (Fig. 7.1). We stopped first at an exhibition space and then at the detention zone to view the guard station and attorney interview room, infirmary, shop, visiting room, prison cells, and yard. We also visited, housed in different buildings, the Military Court and First Court. The tour lasted for just under 1.5 hours and was conducted in English.

There were various interactive elements to the tour that students participated in. They experienced being inside a prison cell and having to crouch to move through an intentionally small door. A student reflected on her conflicting feelings, by showing a picture of a sign: 'It invites you to use shackles as if they were fun. It was conflicting for me to be excited to try them on and have fun, while doing it when I was there to learn about the horrible period of white terror'.[15] It is not easy, another student commented, to enter the museum with your critical glasses on ready to look beyond the narrative of the museum, when actually you are a European with little knowledge of the history to be critical.[16]

Some exchange students were reminded of the history of their own countries. 'In a way, even though our history is very different, Spanish and Taiwanese share approximately 40 years of repression. And although we are from different countries, similar chapters of our different history build a link between us'.[17] A student from Germany selected a picture of the exotic fruits on display in the prison shop. She explained that she chose it because it was the only thing different, everything else was 'eerily similar to Hohenschönhausen prison in Berlin, Germany (...) the exotic fruit [would have been] unthinkable in the former GDR. Terror regimes and political persecution might vary by motivation, but rarely in execution'.[18] Especially as law students, they were affected by seeing these courts as places not 'where rights are recognized and protected, but where rights can be completely disregarded, an instrument to legitimate unjust and discretionary decisions and judgements'.[19]

Beginning the leap of connecting the museum narrative to transnational law, a student reflected: 'Without international law (such as the discourse of human rights), it's impossible to have such a human right museum in Taiwan'.[20] Another student added how the museum 'cleans up the memory of those innocent people who were convicted unjustly. It works as an ambassador of human rights because when we visit a place like this, we realise why human rights are important and why it is important that they are worldwide recognised'.[21] Connecting the museum narrative to Taiwan, they continued:

---

[15] Student written reflection, on file with authors.
[16] Author's discussion notes, on file.
[17] Student written reflection, on file with authors.
[18] Student written reflection, on file with authors.
[19] Student written reflection, on file with authors.
[20] Student written reflection, on file with authors.
[21] Student written reflection, on file with authors.

the museum recalls the international relations of the 1980s. At that time, the KMT began to liberalize Taiwan in order to gain support from the US to prevent military attacks from China. So, I think that international law was used as a kind of bargaining chip to gain an ally. Also, I found that recently the Taiwanese government likes to use the discourse of "First in Asia" to brand Taiwan as the friend of the international community. For example, as the introductory video says, the Human Rights Museum is the first human rights museum in Asia, and it also aimed at educating the values of human rights and democracy to the visitors. (Another example is the legalization of same-sex marriage in 2019).[22]

TAIWAN AND THE WORLD

We view the National Human Rights Museum as a form of alternative diplomacy geared towards advancing Taiwan's self-determination. Even so, the museum and guided tour did not mention the issue of Taiwanese independence explicitly themselves. Instead, we place the narrative of the museum within a longer trajectory of Taiwan appealing to the international to safeguard its place in the world. Very moving was the articulation of the message of the museum by one student: 'we need to do our best and work hard to show we are part of the international community. It is ironic that this happened when we were a UN Member, and now we are not, but we do much better. To prove ourselves worthy of the international community is the big charge of Taiwan'.[23]

It is said that 'Taiwan exists in the between': in between competing discourses of unification on the one hand and ambivalent expressions of independence on the other.[24] The KMT government of the Republic of China (ROC) retreated to Taiwan at the end of the Chinese Civil War in 1949, leaving the Communist Party of China on the Chinese mainland where it founded the People's Republic of China (PRC).[25] Famously, the ROC had a seat at the UN until 1971, when they were replaced by the

---

[22] Student written reflection, on file with authors.

[23] Author's discussion notes, on file.

[24] Funie Hsu, Brian Hioe and Wen Liu, "Collective Statement on Taiwan Independence: Building Global Solidarity and Rejecting US Military Empire" *American Quarterly* 69 no. 3 (2017): 465–568.

[25] See, for example, F. Gilbert Chan (ed.) *China at the Crossroads: Nationalists and Communists, 1927–1949* (New York: Routledge, 2018).

PRC.[26] Whilst the status of Taiwan to this day remains uncertain, the PRC maintains a 'One China' policy, which includes the goal of unification. The status of Taiwan is further complicated by the PRC, which refuses diplomatic relations with countries that recognise the ROC.[27] As a consequence, only 14 UN Member States officially recognise Taiwan.[28] This further complicates international relations for Taiwan, which is largely barred from membership to international organisations. Yet, de facto, many States do maintain various ties with Taiwan under different nomers.

In international law, there are traditionally two theories of recognition of statehood.[29] The first is a declarative theory specifying that an act of recognition of one State by another State is simply to affirm the one State meets the requirements of statehood following from the 1933 Montevideo Convention. The second is a constitutive theory, meant to account for the political element of recognition. With the latter, the emphasis lies with the acceptance of the aspiring State by existing States as member of their political community. Without such recognition, the actual conduct of international relations is seriously complicated. In this sense, recognition is constitutive. The more States recognise an entity as a State, the more likely it will come to constitute one.

In the above, the two theories of recognition stand in opposition. To put this into relief: either an entity is recognised as a State based on objective criteria of statehood, or such recognition depends on the whims of existing States. This distinction can, however, also be questioned, as Rose Parfitt asserts in paraphrasing Hans Kelsen: 'if states are the only "competent authority" available to establish the "fact" of international

---

[26] UNGA resolution 2758 (XXVI) "Restoration of the lawful rights of the People's Republic of China in the United Nations" 25 October 1971. Available: https://digitallibrary.un.org/record/192054?ln=en accessed 7 April 2020.

[27] Ministry of Foreign Affairs Republic of China (Taiwan), "Instances of China's Interference with Taiwan's International Presence, 2020," https://www.mofa.gov.tw/en/cp.aspx?n=AD8BA59033D4F35C.

[28] Belize, Eswati (formerly Swaziland), Guatemala, Haiti, Honduras, Marshall Islands, Nauru, Nicaragua, Palau, Paraguay, Saint Kitts and Nevis, Saint Lucia, Saint Vincent and the Grenadines, and Tuvalu, as well as Holy See.

[29] James Crawford, *The Creation of States in International Law* (Oxford: OUP, 2007); Rose Parfitt, "Theorizing Recognition and International Personality," in *The Oxford Handbook of the Theory of International Law*, ed. Florian Hoffman and Anne Orford (Oxford: OUP, 2016).

personality, then it runs counter to the principle of sovereign equality that recognition [...] could be anything but constitutive'.[30] This is because recognition would always depend on an act of existing States over an entity that is thus not yet a State.

Moreover, Parfitt adds, in the history of would-be States seeking international recognition, 'the short straw seems always to be drawn by the Other'.[31] Conforming to a perceived 'standard of civilization' may help with achieving recognition, even if it is by no means a guarantee. In this light, Taiwan's bid to appear as little 'Other' as possible, presenting itself instead as a liberal and progressive candidate to the international community, seems to be a strategic move in pursuing international recognition, which we see here played out in the theatre of the museum.

Moreover, in the specific context of Taiwan, a strategy of a subtle 'fitting in' seems a less risky route than, for instance, provoking a statement from the international community and particularly from the PRC, with a unilateral declaration of independence. Such a possibility exists insofar as the International Court of Justice (ICJ) notoriously opined that 'the declaration of independence of Kosovo (...) did not violate international law',[32] even if the ICJ in this advisory opinion did not consider the legal consequences of the declaration as these relate to the achievement of statehood, or the validity or legal effects of the recognition of Kosovo by other States.[33] The point to stress here too is that international law itself is uncertain as to when a State is recognised sufficiently to indeed constitute a State.

In international law there are thus different theories of sovereignty and statehood, but in Gerry Simpson's words, it also pays to have a certain 'sleight of hand'.[34] Where international law cannot bring certainty on Taiwan's current status, alternative means of diplomacy are pursued to

[30] Ibid. Parfitt, drawing from: Hans Kelsen, "Recognition in International Law," *American Journal of International Law* 35 (1941): 605–617.

[31] Ibid. Also on the Eurocentric nature of the concepts of sovereignty and civilization: Anthony Anghie, *Imperialism, Sovereignty and the Making of International Law* (Cambridge: CUP, 2004).

[32] International Court of Justice, *Accordance with International Law of the Unilateral Declaration of Independence in Respect of Kosovo ('Kosovo Opinion')*, Advisory Opinion 22 July 2010 (I.C.J. Reports 2010), para. 123(3).

[33] Ibid, para 51.

[34] Gerry Simpson, "Something to Do With States" in ed. Hoffman and Orford supra note 29.

communicate a message from the Taiwanese government. In addition to welcoming representative offices as de facto embassies or consulates in Taiwan, and participating with an observer status or on a non-state basis in international organisations, the government of Taiwan promotes cultural diplomacy. Such cultural diplomacy may take the shape of educational exchange programmes, which many in our study trip are part of—including the teacher. It also takes shape through the communication and remembrance of historic events. As a favoured destination of tourists, museums can be venues for reaching an (international) audience, and for communicating a carefully designed narrative to them.

Complicating matters further, Taiwan remains internally divided on the issue, with its two main political parties differing on a future course towards reunification (KMT) or towards independence (Democratic Progressive Party—DPP). Depending on which political party is in power, the message presented through (alternative) diplomacy may vary.

We view the Museum of White Terror in the light of this alternative diplomacy of sorts, as a way of playing into this 'sleight of hand'. In view of the political agenda of the DPP government that is currently in power and that has explicitly supported the opening of the museum, we understand the message of the museum to be part of an appeal to the international community for a (de facto) recognition of Taiwan. To articulate independent and progressive ownership of Taiwan's political past is part of that appeal.

CHILDREN DON'T TALK POLITICS

Taking ownership of Taiwan's political past, our guided tour through the National Human Rights Museum recalled the history of White Terror. The tour tells the story of 'White Terror', denoting national and systematic action to suppress communist or left-wing activists and political protesters.[35] This period of White Terror lasted for over 40 years, starting in 1949.[36]

After entering the first exhibition room in the prison building, the guide showed us a model of an old detention facility, the Taipei Military Prison. This prison had been so overcrowded after mass arrests in the 1950s that political prisoners were relocated to the Xindian Military Prison in 1968, our current site.[37] Students were shocked by the number of political prisoners held in narrow cells and interrogated here in what is now downtown Taipei.

When the KMT arrived in Taiwan in 1949, they began implementing various kinds of restrictive legislation, including *Martial Law, Temporary Provisions Effective During the Period of National Mobilization for the Suppression of the Communist Rebellion, Statutes for the Punishment of Rebellion*, and *Statutes for the Detection and Eradication of Spies During the Period of Communist Rebellion*.[38] Such statutes extended the authority and presidency of President Chiang Kai-Shek, expanded the elements and punishment of the rebellion under Criminal Law, and enlarged the power for 'public security authorities' to investigate reported communists.[39]

At first, the KMT prohibited people from contacting the Communist Party of China (CPC) and discussing communism. 'Everyone shall protect national security information and counter-espionage' was the political

---

[35] 臺灣白色恐怖時期相關史蹟點調查案總結報告書 [Summary Report on the Investigation of Related Historical Sites during the White Terror Period in Taiwan](New Taipei: National Human Rights Museum Preparation Office, 2015), 3, https://issuu.com/nhrm/docs/_____2f46568fbf7b64; Wakabayashi Masahiro, 戰後臺灣政治史:中華民國臺灣化的歷程 [The "Republic of China" and the Politics of Taiwanization: The Changing Identity of Taiwan in Postwar East Asia], trans. 洪郁如 (Taipei: National Taiwan University Press, 2016), 58.

[36] "White Terror Period: Background", National Human Rights Museum available: https://www.nhrm.gov.tw/en/content_88.html Some mentioned Taiwan entered White terror after the 2–28 incident in 1947, See Tsung-Kuang Lin, *The Taiwanese Identity Question and the "2-28" Incident, An Introduction to 2-28 Tragedy in Taiwan: For World Citizens* (Taipei: Taiwan Renaissance Foundation Press, 1998), 105.

[37] "Historical Sites of Injustice: Taipei Military Prison", National Human Rights Museum, accessed June 3 2020, https://hsi.nhrm.gov.tw/home/en-us/injusticelandmarks-en/301298.

[38] 李筱峰 and 薛化元, 戰後台灣史 [Taiwan's Post-war History] (Taipei: Taiwan Interminds Publishing, 2019), 65–66.

[39] 李筱峰 and 薛化元, *Post-war history*, 83.

Fig. 7.2 'Keep Silent' propaganda message. (Photo: Owen Zong-Syuan Han)

propaganda of the government from the 1950s.[40] White Terror propaganda messages are displayed in the National Human Rights Museum (Fig. 7.2). A student reflected:

> The big words mean "keep silent", and this accurately reflects how human rights violation perpetuates and worsens where there is silence. Silence leads to stagnation, and even regression at times. Non-silence is important for it is active discourse and discussions about it which changes the situation.[41]

The aim of suppressing communists turned into mass oppression of political dissidents and Taiwan independence supporters.[42] People were

---

[40] 陳世昌, 戰後70年台灣史 [70-year history of the post-war Taiwan] (Taipei: China Times Publishing, 2015), 100.

[41] Student written reflection, on file with authors.

[42] Wakabayashi, *Politics of Taiwanization*, 58.

accused for merely exercising freedom of expression, or for advocating their rights. Sometimes people suffered from being wrongly reported. As a result, more than 10,000 people were detained, tortured, and sentenced to prison by military courts of the KMT regime.[43] All of this happened here at Jing-Mei, the site of the present-day White Terror Memorial Park and National Human Rights Museum.

The students' notes bear frequent references to their shock at the unfair trials and inhumane treatment of the prisoners. 'The idea that the military prosecutor, while using a smaller chair than the judges is still on the same bench is unnerving. This highlighted the lack of a judicial process', one student wrote.[44] Students also noted how in the prisons at Jing-Mei, people's movement was limited, their food was cut apart for examination, and the only source of water in the cells was from the toilet.[45] One student notes how prisoners could not talk about their cases and treatment in the jail, 'but they still tried hard to convey messages to the outside, calling for international support. [...] International law helps pull up the human rights standards in Taiwan, and helps Taiwan to gradually move to democracy'.[46] Getting a message out was crucial, as at the time, people did not know that Jing-Mei was a political prison.[47] Even now, not all archives have been opened.[48]

'Children don't talk politics' is what parents and elders still admonish youth in Taiwan.[49] In Taiwan, the generations born after the 1990s, the period during which the democratisation process of Taiwan rapidly

---

[43] 胡慧玲, 百年追求: 臺灣民主運動的故事卷三-民主的浪潮 [A Century of Pursuit: The Story of Taiwan Democracy Movement Volume Three: The Wave of Democracy] (New Taipei: Acropolis, 2013), 23–26.

[44] Student written reflection, on file with authors.

[45] Taken from three student written reflections, on file with authors.

[46] Student written reflection, on file with authors.

[47] See the oral history of Tsai Tsai-Yuan: 蔡財源, "坐黑牢也爭正義 [Sit in jail and fight for justice]," in 走過長夜: 政治受難者的生命故事, 輯二, 看到陽光的時候 [*Walking Through the Long Night: The Life Stories of Political Victims, Part Two: When I See the Sunlight*], ed. 周佩蓉 et al (New Taipei: National Human Rights Museum preparation office, 2015), 189–193.

[48] The Political Archives Act was passed in 2019, and the declassification of files is still ongoing by administration; Yu Hsiang, Wang Yang-yu and Emerson Lim, "Taiwan's parliament passes bill on declassifying political files", *Focus Taiwan CNA English News*, July 24, 2019, https://focustaiwan.tw/politics/201907040022; see also "Political Archives Act", National Archives Administration, last modified July 24, 2019, https://www.archives.gov.tw/English/Publish.aspx?cnid=103930.

[49] 簡永達, "尋找政治隱傷者 – 那些受難者、他們的家人、還有我們 [Looking for Political Victims – Those Victims, Their Families, and Us]", *The Reporter*, February 27, 2017, https://www.twreporter.org/a/228-political-victims-families.

unfolded, typically have a very different perspective on history, memory, national identity, and political ideology than more senior generations who lived through the experience of White Terror. This division between younger and older generations is reflected in the support for the two main political parties, the KMT and the DPP, for whom the interpretation of history and the status of Taiwan are high on their agendas. The National Human Rights Museum itself, supported by the DPP, which in turn is largely supported by the younger generation, delivers a strong message on both these issues.

Four decades of 'White Terror' cast a profound spell on people, who became silent about political and social issues.[50] The historical memory instilled a fear of discussing politics and views on the Taiwanese status in older generations in Taiwan. By contrast, generations born after the end of the 'White Terror' period are willing to participate in politics and increasingly identify themselves as Taiwanese. From 1991 to 1994, President Lee Teng-hui gradually led the KMT to abolish the repressive laws of the White Terror period, and in 1996 he implemented the first direct presidential elections.[51] This 'quiet revolution' laid the foundation for Taiwan's democratisation.[52] The generation born after 1990 has been educated and grown up in a democratic environment and has enjoyed freedom of speech and political participation. In addition, this younger generation is no longer instilled with the 'Chinese' identity.[53] Instead, 83% of people aged under 30 see themselves as 'Taiwanese'.[54] In Taiwan, they

[50] See "White Terror Period," National Human Rights Museum, accessed April 2, 2020, https://www.nhrm.gov.tw/en/content_88.html.

[51] Wakabayashi, *Politics of Taiwanization*, 218–222.

[52] Lee Teng-hui, *The Road to Democracy: Taiwan's Pursuit of Identity* (Tokyo: PHP Institute, Inc., 1999), 125–126.

[53] See the Taiwanese government report: Presidential Office Indigenous Historical Justice and Transitional Justice Committee, Subcommittee on Languages, "中華民國政府漢化政策下不當限制族語使用的歷史真相: 政府文書、口述訪談初探 報告文稿 [The Historical Truth of Improperly Restricting the Use of Ethnic Languages under the Chinazation Policy of the Government of the Republic of China]", September 28, 2019, 3.: "The KMT government published the "strengthening the implementation of national language project" which forces all ethics in Taiwan into speaking Mandarin instead of their own dialect in order to " inculcate the motherland's culture and enhance national identity."

[54] Kat Delvin and Christine Huang, "In Taiwan, Views of Mainland China Mostly Negative," *Pew Research Center*, May 12, 2020, https://www.pewresearch.org/global/2020/05/12/in-taiwan-views-of-mainland-china-mostly-negative/.

are known as the 'born independence' generation.[55] For them, speaking out on Taiwan's past and forging an independent status for Taiwan are key issues.

The very uncertainty over Taiwan's legal status offers room for different interpretations on these key issues and leaves the consensus open as to how history is presented. This is reflected in the fact that the national status and interpretation of history are the main controversies of the two major political parties. The KMT and its supporters play down the emphasis on White Terror and instead commemorate and commend the former leader Chiang Kai-shek for combating communism. They advocate that the ROC regime represents the 'whole China', that is, Taiwan as part of China, yet ideally under KMT rule. Their rival party, the DPP and its voters, emphasise the need for transitional justice after the authoritarian era and the value of the history of democratic transformation, and take the stance of a Taiwanese national awareness and ultimately independence.

In advancing their respective political agendas, both parties have resorted to exerting power over and through symbols, memorials, and education. The magnificent Chiang Kai-shek Memorial Hall in the centre of Taipei changed names to 'Taiwan Democracy Memorial Hall' in 2007 under the DPP.[56] The name change was reverted in 2009, when the KMT took office again.[57] In 2015, the KMT government adjusted the history curriculum to the Chinese interpretation of history,[58] which triggered large-scale protests by high school students.[59] After DPP's Tsai Ing-wen

---

[55] Anna Fifield, "Taiwan's 'Born Independent' Millennials are Becoming Xi Jinping's Lost Generation," *Washington Post*, December 26, 2019, https://www.washingtonpost.com/world/asia_pacific/taiwans-born-independent-millennials-are-becoming-xi-jinpings-lost-generation/2019/12/24/ce1da5c8-20d5-11ea-9c2b-060477c13959_story.html.

[56] Under DPP President Chen Shui-bian. See: Jimmy Chuang, "Name fight set for CKS Memorial Hall," *Taipei Times* May 10, 2007, http://www.taipeitimes.com/News/front/archives/2007/05/10/2003360233; Jenny W. Hsu, "Inscription goes up at Democracy Hall," *Taipei Times*, November 7, 2007, https://www.taipeitimes.com/News/front/archives/2007/12/09/2003391782.

[57] Flora Wang, "Chiang Kai-shek plaque to return to memorial hall," *Taipei Times*, January 22, 2009, http://www.taipeitimes.com/News/taiwan/archives/2009/01/22/2003434392.

[58] Under KMT President Ma Ying-jeou. See: Loa Iok-sin and Jake Chung, "Ministry approves new 'brainwashing' curriculum," *Taipei Times*, July 28, 2014, http://www.taipeitimes.com/News/front/archives/2014/01/28/2003582309; Sean Lin, "Curriculum Protests: No extra emphasis on China: MOE," *Taipei Times*, July 25, 2015 http://www.taipeitimes.com/News/taiwan/archives/2015/07/25/2003623857.

[59] Sean Lin, "Students rally against altered curricula," *Taipei Times*, July 6, 2015, https://www.taipeitimes.com/News/front/archives/2015/07/06/2003622364.

was elected president in 2016, she immediately withdrew the KMT version of the history curriculum.[60] President Tsai Ing-wen also established the Transitional Justice Committee in 2018 to reflect on history and promote transitional justice.[61] This is just to show how historical interpretation and national identity are still highly controversial and entangled issues in Taiwan. The memorial park too has gone through several naming disputes between the DPP and KMT, alternately emphasising and watering down the 'human rights' element.[62] Though a preparatory office was formed in 2011,[63] the National Human Rights Museum was not formally established until the DPP took office again in 2016.

After our tour of the museum, one student shared her picture of a display showing a shared meal laid out in one of the prison cells. There is a humanity in sharing dinner, she said, and to do so under these circumstances fosters a bond that lasts beyond this prison.[64] Her statement is of special significance for the DPP. The DPP first took power in 2000, with the election of President Chen Shui-bian and Vice President Lu Xiu-Lian.[65] Their connection to the Jing-Mei prison is very personal. Ms Lu herself was detained here and[66] at that time Mr. Chen had been her lawyer.[67] At the end of President Chen's administration in 2007, he

---

[60] Sean Lin, "Guideline changes to be undone," *Taipei Times*, May 22, 2016, https://www.taipeitimes.com/News/front/archives/2016/05/22/2003646821.

[61] "President Tsai presides over inauguration ceremony for Transitional Justice Commission," Republic of China (Taiwan) Office of the President, News Release May 31, 2018, accessed April 15, 2020, https://english.president.gov.tw/NEWS/5418.

[62] Loa Iok-sin, "Activists mobilize to stop changes to Jingmei park," *Taipei Times*, April 24, 2009 http://www.taipeitimes.com/News/taiwan/archives/2009/04/24/2003441903.

[63] "副總統出席國家人權博物館籌備處揭牌活動 [Vice President attended the unveiling of the preparatory office of the National Museum of Human Rights]," Republic of China (Taiwan) Office of the President, News Release December 10, 2011, accessed April 15, 2020, https://www.president.gov.tw/NEWS/16179.

[64] Student written reflection, on file with authors.

[65] Erik Eckholm, "Taiwan's New Leader Ends Decades of Nationalist Rule," *New York Times*, May 20, 2000, https://www.nytimes.com/2000/05/20/world/taiwan-s-new-leader-ends-decades-of-nationalist-rule.html.

[66] Following the Kaohsiung Incident in 1979. See: 陳世宏 and 何靜茹, "紀念美麗島事件30週年影像史 [A video History Commemorating the 30th Anniversary of the Kaohsiung Incident], in 美麗島30週年研究論文集 [Collection of Research Papers on the 30th Anniversary of Kaohsiung Incident], ed. 張炎憲 and 陳朝海 (Taipei: 吳三連台灣史料基金會, 2010), 60.

[67] 陳世宏and何靜茹, "A video History," 63.

reorganised the former Jing-Mei Military detention centre into the Jing-Mei Human Rights Park.

CONCLUSION

Going through the guided tour was just like walking through the history and struggle of Taiwan's democracy. Our tour ended in the courtroom where the trial of Ms Lu concerning the Kaohsiung Incident had taken place in 1980. Our guide told us that the trial was symbolic in that it gained international attention, promoted the democratic activists, and accelerated the end of the authoritarian period.

Preparations for the opening of the museum have been closely linked to Taiwan's process of democratisation. Through the exhibition at the museum, the government demonstrates support for transitional justice and democracy. The museum not only preserves the country's historical memory but also conveys a message to the international community and to foreign visitors with the support of the government. On the occasion of International Human Rights Day 2016, DPP president Tsai Ing-wen asserted in Jing-Mei Memorial Park:

> In addition to recovering the historical truth, we must also present our findings publicly via publications, art, films, and other media, so that more people will understand the White Terror period. And, most important of all, critically examining the system of oppression and thinking hard about justice ought to become a mass movement in our society, so that we can build up a set of shared values and goals.[68]

Through guided tours and exhibitions, visitors, whether native or foreign, can feel the message delivered from here: Taiwan is independent in democracy, human rights, and transitional justice.

Looking at the Museum of White Terror as a transnational legal actor of sorts posits its historical narrative presented through specifically its guided tour within a complex political landscape. We contend that where international law cannot resolve the question of Taiwan's status, the museum becomes a means of alternative diplomacy in pursuit of an answer. Placing the narrative of the guided tour within the prominent wider

---

[68] "President Tsai attends activities to mark International Human Rights Day 2016," Republic of China (Taiwan) Office of the President, News Release December 10, 2016, accessed April 12, 2020, https://english.president.gov.tw/NEWS/5043.

context of Taiwan's self-determination, we view the story of the museum as a way of establishing Taiwan's sovereignty over its past and future, and therefore ultimately as a plea for independence.

We have encountered the narrative of the museum as a group, and we have reconstructed it based on our own reflections and those of our students. We close the story with a reflection and photograph collected by our group.

> I chose this picture because of the guide emphasising the ironic decision of putting a lion, symbol of strength and freedom, in front of the entrance of a political jail. This also symbolizes the relationship between past and present and of the important duty of memory. At the transnational law level, it also has an impact under the actual Taiwan political situation perspective. Because Taiwan has lived through such trouble to gain the democracy it has today, it would be great to recognize it as an official state everywhere in the world.

Fig. 7.3 Students pass the statue of a lion created and donated by a former prisoner standing in front of the prison entrance. The characters on the prison façade read: 'collaborate & fight the enemy'. (Photo: Renske Vos)

This combined with the message sent here which is also to memorize traumatic events at the international level is what this picture tells me.[69] (Fig. 7.3)

BIBLIOGRAPHY

Anghie, Anthony. 2004. *Imperialism, Sovereignty and the Making of International Law*. Cambridge: CUP.

Apsel, Joyce. 2016. *Introducing Peace Museums*. London: Routledge.

Belavusau, Ulad, and Aleksandra Gliszczyńska-Grabias, eds. 2017. *Memory: Towards Legal Governance of History*. Cambridge: CUP.

Bernstein, Anya. 2008. The Social Life of Regulation in Taipei City Hall: The Role of Legality in the Administrative Bureaucracy. *Law & Social Inquiry* 33 (4): 925–954.

Chan, F. Gilbert, ed. 2018. *China at the Crossroads: Nationalists and Communists, 1927–1949*. New York: Routledge.

Chuang, Jimmy. Name Fight Set for CKS Memorial Hall. *Taipei Times*, 10 May 2007. Accessed 15 April 2020. http://www.taipeitimes.com/News/front/archives/2007/05/10/2003360233.

Clark, Janine. 2013. Reconciliation Through Remembrance? War Memorials and the Victims of Vukovar. *International Journal of Transitional Justice* 7 (1): 116–135.

Crawford, James. 2007. *The Creation of States in International Law*. Oxford: OUP.

Eckholm, Erik. Taiwan's New Leader Ends Decades of Nationalist Rule. *New York Times*, 20 May 2000. Accessed 14 April 2020. https://www.nytimes.com/2000/05/20/world/taiwan-s-new-leader-ends-decades-of-nationalist-rule.html.

Fifield, Anna. Taiwan's 'born independent' Millennials Are Becoming Xi Jinping's Lost Generation. *Washington Post*, 26 December 2019. Accessed 15 April 2020. https://www.washingtonpost.com/world/asia_pacific/taiwans-born-independent-millennials-are-becoming-xi-jinpings-lost-generation/2019/12/24/ce1da5c8-20d5-11ea-9c2b-060477c13959_story.html.

Hsu, Funie, Brian Hioe, and Wen Liu. 2017. Collective Statement on Taiwan Independence: Building Global Solidarity and Rejecting US Military Empire. *American Quarterly* 69 (3): 465–568.

Hsu, Jenny. Inscription Goes Up at Democracy Hall. *Taipei Times*, 7 November 2007. Accessed 15 April 2020. https://www.taipeitimes.com/News/front/archives/2007/12/09/2003391782.

---

[69] Student written reflection, on file with authors.

Jao, Nicole. 'Mask Diplomacy' a Boost for Taiwan. *Foreign Policy*, 13 April 2020. Accessed 22 May 2020. https://foreignpolicy.com/2020/04/13/taiwan-coronavirus-pandemic-mask-soft-power-diplomacy/.

Delvin, Kat, and Christine Huang. In Taiwan, Views of Mainland China Mostly Negative. *Pew Research Center*, 12 May 2020. https://www.pewresearch.org/global/2020/05/12/in-taiwan-views-of-mainland-china-mostly-negative/.

Kelsen, Hans. 1941. Recognition in International Law. *American Journal of International Law* 35: 605–617.

Lee, Teng-hui. 1999. *The Road to Democracy: Taiwan's Pursuit of Identity*. Tokyo: PHP Institute, Inc.

Lennon, John, and Malcolm Foley. 2000. *Dark Tourism: The Attraction of Death and Disaster*. London: Thomson.

Lin, Sean. Guideline Changes to Be Undone. *Taipei Times*, 22 May 2016. Accessed 15 April 2020. https://www.taipeitimes.com/News/front/archives/2016/05/22/2003646821.

———. Students Rally Against Altered Curricula. *Taipei Times*, 6 July 2015a. Accessed 15 April 2020. https://www.taipeitimes.com/News/front/archives/2015/07/06/2003622364.

———. Curriculum Protests: No Extra Emphasis on China. *Taipei Times*, 25 July 2015b. Accessed 15 April 2020. http://www.taipeitimes.com/News/taiwan/archives/2015/07/25/2003623857.

Lin, Tsung-Kuang. 1998. *The Taiwanese Identity Question and the "2-28" Incident, An Introduction to 2-28 Tragedy in Taiwan: For World Citizens*. Taipei: Taiwan Renaissance Foundation Press.

Lisle, Debbie, and Heather Johnson. 2018. Lost in the Aftermath. *Security Dialogue* 50 (1): 20–39.

Loa, Iok-sin. Activists Mobilize to Stop Changes to Jingmei Park. *Taipei Times*, 24 April 2009. Accessed 16 April 2020. http://www.taipeitimes.com/News/taiwan/archives/2009/04/24/2003441903.

Loa, Iok-sin, and Jake Chung. Ministry Approves New 'brainwashing' Curriculum. *Taipei Times*, 28 July 2014. Accessed 15 April 2020. http://www.taipeitimes.com/News/front/archives/2014/01/28/2003582309.

Ministry of Foreign Affairs Republic of China (Taiwan). Instances of China's Interference with Taiwan's International Presence, 2020. *Policies & Issues*. Accessed June 5, 2020. https://www.mofa.gov.tw/en/cp.aspx?n=AD8BA59033D4F35C.

National Archives Administration. Political Archives Act. https://www.archives.gov.tw/English/Publish.aspx?cnid=103930. Last Modified July 24, 2019.

National Human Rights Museum. 國家人權博物館白色恐怖景美紀念園區簡介 [Introduction to the White Horror Jingmei Memorial Park of the National Museum of Human Rights(EN)]. Video zone. Accessed 24 March 2020. https://www.nhrm.gov.tw/en/movie_85_3874.html.

———. 2015. 臺灣白色恐怖時期相關史蹟點調查案總結報告書 [Summary Report on the Investigation of Related Historical Sites during the White Terror Period in Taiwan]. New Taipei: National Human Rights Museum Preparation Office. https://issuu.com/nhrm/docs/_____ ____2f46568fbf7b64.

Parfitt, Rose. 2016. Theorizing Recognition and International Personality. In *The Oxford Handbook of the Theory of International Law*, ed. Florian Hoffman and Anne Orford. Oxford: OUP.

Presidential Office Indigenous Historical Justice and Transitional Justice Committee, Subcommittee on Languages. *中華民國政府漢化政策下不當限制族語使用的歷史真相:政府文書、口述訪談初探 報告文稿* [The Historical Truth of Improperly Restricting the Use of Ethnic Languages under the Chinesization Policy of the Government of the Republic of China]. September 28, 2019.

Republic of China (Taiwan) Office of the President. 副總統出席國家人權博物館籌備處揭牌活動 [Vice President Attended the Unveiling of the Preparatory Office of the National Museum of Human Rights]. News Release. December 10, 2011. Accessed April 15, 2020. https://www.president.gov.tw/NEWS/16179.

———. President Tsai Presides Over Inauguration Ceremony for Transitional Justice Commission. News Release. May 31, 2018. Accessed April 15, 2020. https://english.president.gov.tw/NEWS/5418.

———. President Tsai Attends Activities to Mark International Human Rights Day 2016. News Release. December 10, 2016. Accessed April 12, 2020. https://english.president.gov.tw/NEWS/5043.

Roodenburg, Lisa, and Sofia Stolk. 2020. The Desire to Be an International Law City: A Self-Portrait of The Hague and Amsterdam. In *International Law's Collected Stories*, ed. Sofia Stolk and Renske Vos. London: Palgrave.

Simpson, Gerry. 2016. Something to Do With States. In *The Oxford Handbook of the Theory of International Law*, ed. Florian Hoffman and Anne Orford. Oxford: OUP.

Stolk, Sofia, and Renske Vos. 2020. International Legal Sightseeing. *Leiden Journal of International Law* 33 (1): 1–11.

Wang, Flora. Chiang Kai-shek Plaque to Return to Memorial Hall. Taipei Times, 22 January 2009. Accessed 14 April 2020. http://www.taipeitimes.com/News/taiwan/archives/2009/01/22/2003434392.

Wang, Hsin-yu, and Joseph Yeh. Crowdfunded 'Taiwan can help' Ad Published in New York Times. *Focus Taiwan* (CNA English News), 14 April 2020. Accessed 25 May 2020.

Wakabayashi Masahiro. *戰後臺灣政治史: 中華民國臺灣化的歷程* [The "Republic of China" and the Politics of Taiwanization: The Changing Identity of Taiwan in Postwar East Asia]. Translated by 洪郁如. Taipei: National Taiwan University Press, 2016.

Yu Hsiang, Wang Yang-yu, and Emerson Lim. Taiwan's Parliament Passes Bill on Declassifying Political Files. *Focus Taiwan CNA English News*, July 24, 2019. https://focustaiwan.tw/politics/201907040022.

李筱峰 and 薛化元, 戰後台灣史 [Taiwan's Post-war History]. 2019. Taipei: Taiwan Interminds Publishing.

胡慧玲, 百年追求: 臺灣民主運動的故事卷三-民主的浪潮 [A Century of Pursuit: The Story of Taiwan Democracy Movement Volume Three: The Wave of Democracy]. 2013. New Taipei: Acropolis.

陳世宏 and 何靜茹. 2010. 紀念美麗島事件30週年影像史[A Video History Commemorating the 30th Anniversary of the Kaoshiung Incident]. In 美麗島 30週年研究論文集 [*Collection of Research Papers on the 30th Anniversary of Kaoshiung Incident*], ed. 張炎憲 and 陳朝海, 40–66. Taipei: 吳三連台灣史料基金會.

陳世昌. 2015. 戰後70年台灣史 [*70-Year History of the Post-war Taiwan*]. Taipei: China Times Publishing.

陳齊奐 (Qi-Huan Tan). 景美人權文化園區的導覽敘事與人權教育初探 [Study on the Narrative Structure and Human Rights Education of the Jing-Mei Human Rights Memorial and Cultural Park]. *Museology Quarterly*, 28 (3) (July 2014): 87–110. https://doi.org/10.6686/MuseQ.201407_28(3).0006.

蔡財源. 2015. 坐黑牢也爭正義 [Sit in Jail and Fight for Justice]. In 走過長夜:政治受難者的生命故事, 輯二, 看到陽光的時候 [*Walking Through the Long Night: The Life Stories of Political Victims, Part Two: When I See the Sunlight*], ed. 周佩蓉 et al., 179–196. New Taipei: National Human Rights Museum Preparation Office.

簡永達. 尋找政治隱傷者 – 那些受難者、他們的家人, 還有我們 [Looking for Political Victims – Those Victims, Their Families, and Us]. *The Reporter*, February 27, 2017. https://www.twreporter.org/a/228-political-victims-families.

CHAPTER 8

Becoming Epilogual

Gerry Simpson

The field of law and literature has, by now, a quite lengthy history. Lawyers, on one of their customary cross-border incursions, have visited literature for fresh resources (think of Ed Morgan's *The Aesthetics of International Law*, his book-length plea for a new self-conscious international law and an exercise in what we might call comparative law and literature), while literary theorists have—more occasionally—taken a tolerant interest in legal writing.[1] Early law and literature was very canonical (often involving a survey of favourite books for fresh depictions of legal process (*Bleak House*) or concepts of usury (*The Merchant of Venice*)).[2] At other times, lawyers and literary scholars have slugged it out over the appropriate way

---

[1] An earlyish classic is Robin West, *Narrative, Authority and Law* (Ann Arbor: University of Michigan Press, 1993). Or from the literature side, Julie Peters, "Law, Literature and the Vanishing Real," *PMLA* 120, no. 2 (2005): 442–453. See Ed Morgan, *Aesthetics of International Law* (Toronto: University of Toronto Press, 2007).

[2] See, for example, Richard Posner, *Law and Literature* (Cambridge, MA: Harvard University Press, 1988). For a recent, elegant survey see Andrea Bianchi, *International Law Theories: An Inquiry into Different Ways of Thinking* (Oxford: Oxford University Press, 2016), 289–291.

G. Simpson (✉)
London School of Economics and Political Science, London, UK
e-mail: g.j.simpson@lse.ac.uk

S. Stolk, R. Vos (eds.), *International Law's Collected Stories*,
Palgrave Studies in International Relations,
https://doi.org/10.1007/978-3-030-58835-9_8

137

to enagage with text.[3] Christopher Warren and Chenxi Tang, meanwhile, approach the history of international law (or the law of nations) as a history of literature, with the sorts of inclinations one might expect from literary scholars.[4] Alongside this there have been bold efforts to treat international law as a language: to think about authorial will and intention, rhetorical device, grammar, meaning, and so on.[5] But we have witnessed, more recently, an effort to transcend these familiar relations of law and literature and produce something more experimental, less canonesque, decentred, even decolonised.[6] In her keynote to a 2019 *Conference on International Law and Literature at the Edge*, Maria Aristodemou called for a disruptive relationship, perhaps even bad relations, between law and literature, and this ethos underpins work by Joseph Slaughter, Christopher Gevers and many others. And now we have a turn to narrative, to the tales international lawyers tell themselves about their discipline.

It is in this disruptive context that Sofia and Renske have asked me to write an epilogue to their marvellous arrangement of stories about international law. I am touched and honoured, and worried. You see, this is my third epilogue of the year. In the old days—also, the young days—I would be asked to write actual essays: full-blooded, multi-footnote affairs crammed with substance and coming in at a healthy 10—15,000 words. When (and why) did I become epilogual? And how long is an epilogue supposed to be? Recently, I attended a writing retreat with my daughters, Hanna and Rosa. At a certain point, we were asked to read aloud our stories, about "objects of affection". My object was a jumper belonging to

---

[3] Stanley Fish, "Working on the Chain Gang: Interpretation in the Law and in Literary Criticism," *Critical Inquiry* 9, no. 1 (1982): 201; Stanley Fish, "Still Wrong after All These Years," *Law and Philosophy* 6, no. 3 (1987): 401; Ronald Dworkin, "My Reply to Stanley Fish (and Walter Benn Michaels): Please Don't Talk About Objectivity Anymore," in *The Politics of Interpretation*, ed. WJT Mitchell (Chicago: Chicago University Press, 1983). See, too, in a productive and contemporaneous counter-move, Robert Cover, "Foreword: Narrative and Nomos," *Harvard Law Review* 97, no. 4 (1983): 4.

[4] Christopher Warren, *Literature and the Law of Nations, 1580–1680* (Oxford: Oxford University Press, 2015); Chenxi Tang, *Imagining World Order: Literature and International Law in Early Modern Europe, 1500–1800* (Ithaca: Cornell University Press, 2018).

[5] On interpretation in international law, see Ingo Venzke, *How Interpretation Makes International Law: On Semantic Change And Normative Twists* (Oxford: Oxford University Press, 2014).

[6] *International Law and Literature at the Edge Project* (Christopher Gevers, Joseph Slaughter, Vasuki Nesiah, Gerry Simpson): Conferences in New York City (Gallatin School) December, 2018; London (LSE), July 2019; Nairobi, forthcoming, 2020).

my oldest friend but the story began with a long disquisition on the many words used to describe "jumpers". As I began performing this little masterpiece, I overheard from the end of the table one of them saying, *sotto voce*, "he's gone meta". So, here I am, writing about epilogues in the epilogue to a book that itself, in these epilogual times, possesses an epilogual mood.

The epilogue comes late in the book in a kind of late-style. An epilogue isn't expected to gloss the contents of the book (this is superbly and lightly accomplished by the editors). If the form permitted it, I would be able to sing the praises of my friend, Mark Drumbl, and his characteristically playful and informed story about the Kapos, or quote from Elisabeth Schweiger and Aoife O'Leary McNiece's creatively Austenian account of international law's evasions and silencings or Thomas Charman's centring of the male victim of war-time (sexual) violence as a corrective to some more emblematic perpetrator—victim images or Lisa Roodenberg's and Sofia Stolk's delicate examination of the self-representations of The Hague and Amsterdam as, respectively, the cities of peace and justice, and human rights or Miha Marcenko's reconstruction of the ideal city as seen through the frame of the UN's Habitat Conference, or Zong-Syuan Han's and Renske Vos's memorable travelogue about a study trip to the Jing-Mei White Terror Memorial Park and the National Human Rights Museum in Taipei: all of this is truly an inspired *mélange* (to re-deploy the editors' apposite term for all of these essays and their various interactions and counteractions).

So, if this fails as conclusion can it succeed as coda? Epilogues seem largely positional as much as anything else, ending where prologues begin, or ending after endings end. But not always. In the *Post Card*, Derrida is forever not quite ending. Even the postscript to *Post Card* is not the ending to the book; two essays follow it. Then again, in *Anti-Oedipus*, Deleuze and Guattari have an introduction that begins in the middle. This epilogue at least ends at the end.

In the *Oxford Handbook of International Criminal Law*, my epilogue was the only essay in a section called "Futures". I predicted in it that international criminal justice had no future and that the future probably didn't have a future either. Judging by these essays, though, international law has a future, and this future has a style. Its style, is, of course, late-style. In "Thoughts on Late Style", Edward Said examines two creative arcs for artists in their late maturity. In one the artist produces fully realised work, crowning masterpieces.[7] Said invokes here Shakespeare's mature later works and Bach's late violin concertos and we can think of others (Robert Lowell, Leonard Cohen, Rembrandt). But late maturity (old age is another term for this) can result in a disruptive, contradictory, cussed, late-style. Said's representatives here are Beethoven (the Ninth Symphony) and Ibsen's final plays. Again, we might think of *Finnegan's Wake* or Charlie Mingus or Philip Roth's nocturnal quartet of short, uncertain, novels. In this sort of work, Said, borrowing from Adorno, argues that there is a splintered, discontinuous, overabundance. The work feels incomplete (of course, sometimes it is incomplete: Kafka, Faulkner, Mozart). In late-style, there is only a kind of void, or "negation", and this void represents the absence of humanity or the idea of creating a different world. As Adorno puts it there is, in this sort of art, "no concession to that would-be humanitarianism to see it through". Said characterises *The Leopard* as one of Europe's great late-style literary artefacts in its refusal to offer redemption for the Sicilian project (through bourgeois self-improvement, peasant revolt, national unity, aristocratic revivalism) and in its portrayal of its protagonist, Don Fabrizio, as he dies, without hope and alongside his aristocratic lineage. These modernist late-styles offer repetition but not redemption. In the end there is nothing but the story; certainly nothing resembling a message. Towards the end of Said's essay, he discusses the modern Greek poet, Cavafy: "In Cavafy, then, the future does not occur, or if it does, it has in a sense already happened....better the internalised, narrow world of limited expectations than that of the grandiose projects constantly betrayed or traduced".[8]

All of this will be familiar to scholars and practitioners of international law. Coming hot on the heels of international law's mature resolutions in the 1990s (the WTO, the New World Order, the Gulf War, the Rome Statute, Investment Arbitration) has been a series of dissipated late-styles. The two beliefs that have sustained modern international lawyers, humanitarianism and the enemy of humankind, have withered: "there are no barbarians any longer...they were, these people, a kind of solution".[9]

---

[7] Edward Said, "Thoughts on Late-Style," *London Review of Books* 26, no. 15 (2004).

[8] Also a book, Edward Said, *On Late-Style: Music and Literature Against the Grain* (New York: Pantheon Books, 2006).

[9] Constantine Cavafy, "Waiting for the Barbarians" (1904). See, too, J.M. Coetzee: "In private I observed that once in every generation, without fail, there is an episode of hysteria about the barbarians...show me a barbarian army and I will believe", *Waiting for the Barbarians* (Philadelphia: Raven Press, 1980): 8.

In light of all this, David Kennedy had already declared *From Apology to Utopia* as "The Last Treatise" and it is not a stretch to think of the past two decades or so as a sequence of last gasp late-styles or afterlives in which the mood is largely fragmentary, allusive, downcast, agitated, and in which the scholarship has become notational, marginal, insecure, dissatisfied. The work, as Said diagnosed, has become rather inventive, if often bleak: *International Law's Objects, International Law's Events, Concepts of International Law*—anything but international law's international law. With the abolition of the future, we now renounce programme for play, subject for story, *nomos* for narrative.[10] And into the breach steps *The Stories of International Law*, this vibrant assortment of late-style tales of the unexpected: a marvellously new international law, so very timely and so very late in the day.

REFERENCES

Bianchi, Andrea. 2016. *International Law Theories: An Inquiry into Different Ways of Thinking*. Oxford: Oxford University Press.

Boer, Lianne. 2019. Narratives of Force: The Presence of the Writer in International Legal Scholarship. *Netherlands International Law Review* 66 (1): 1–20.

Cavafy, Constantine. 1904. Waiting for the Barbarians.

Coetzee, J.M. 1980. *Waiting for the Barbarians*. Philadelphia: Raven Press.

Cover, Robert. 1983. Foreword: Narrative and Nomos. *Harvard Law Review* 97 (4): 4–68.

Dworkin, Ronald. 1983. My Reply to Stanley Fish (and Walter Benn Michaels): Please Don't Talk about Objectivity Anymore. In *The Politics of Interpretation*, ed. W.J.T. Mitchell. Chicago: Chicago University Press.

Fish, Stanley. 1982. Working on the Chain Gang: Interpretation in the Law and in Literary Criticism. *Critical Inquiry* 9 (1): 201–216.

———. 1987. Still Wrong after All These Years. *Law and Philosophy* 6 (3): 401–418.

Gaita, Raimond. 2011. Literature, Genocide, and the Philosophy of International Law. In *Crime, Punishment and Responsibility*, ed. Rowan Cruft, Matthew Kramer, and Mark Reiff. Oxford: Oxford University Press.

---

[10] See Raimond Gaita, "Literature, Genocide, and the Philosophy of International Law," in *Crime, Punishment and Responsibility*, eds. Rowan Cruft, Matthew Kramer & Mark Reiff (Oxford: Oxford University Press, 2011); Lianne Boer, "Narratives of Force: The Presence of the Writer in International Legal Scholarship," *Netherlands International Law Review*, 66, no. 1 (2019); Gerry Simpson, *The Sentimental Life of International Law* (forthcoming, 2021).

Morgan, Ed. 2007. *Aesthetics of International Law*. Toronto: University of Toronto Press.

Peters, Julie. 2005. Law, Literature and the Vanishing Real. *PMLA* 120 (2): 442–453.

Posner, Richard. 1988. *Law and Literature*. Cambridge, MA: Harvard University Press.

Said, Edward. 2004. Thoughts on Late-Style. *London Review of Books* 26 (15).

———. 2006. *On Late-Style: Music and Literature Against the Grain*. New York: Pantheon Books.

Simpson, Gerry. 2021. *The Sentimental Life of International Law*. Forthcoming.

Tang, Chenxi. 2018. *Imagining World Order: Literature and International Law in Early Modern Europe, 1500–1800*. Ithaca: Cornell University Press.

Venzke, Ingo. 2014. *How Interpretation Makes International Law: On Semantic Change And Normative Twists*. Oxford: Oxford University Press.

Warren, Christopher. 2015. *Literature and the Law of Nations, 1580–1680*. Oxford: Oxford University Press.

West, Robin. 1993. *Narrative, Authority and Law*. Ann Arbor: University of Michigan Press.

Printed by Printforce, the Netherlands